DANTON

DANTON

Norman Hampson

Duckworth

To Richard Cobb
with affection and gratitude

First published in 1978 by
Gerald Duckworth & Co. Ltd
The Old Piano Factory
43 Gloucester Crescent, London NW1

© 1978 by Norman Hampson

ISBN 0 7156 1281 6

British Library Cataloguing in Publication Data

Hampson, Norman
    Danton.
    1. Danton, Georges Jacques   2. France – History –
Revolution, 1789–1799 – Biography
    3. Revolutionists – France – Biography
    944.04'092'4   DC146.D2

    ISBN 0–7156–1281–6

Printed in Great Britain by
Bristol Typesetting Co. Ltd
Barton Manor, St Philips
Bristol

Contents

Contents

Preface

It is difficult to write a conventional biography of any of the leaders of the French Revolution. The private papers, diaries, letters to friends and so forth, that help the historian to penetrate beyond the public façade, are almost always lacking. In the case of Danton, these difficulties become virtually insuperable. His reluctance to put anything on paper was notorious and what he did write has been lost or destroyed. Most of the orators of the Revolution took great pains over their speeches, which they read from manuscripts that could be passed on to friendly newspapers or were sometimes published at the expense of the various Assemblies. Danton invariably improvised. On the occasions when his eloquence turned the whole course of a debate, we have probably got a reasonably accurate record of what he said. More often the press gave him less attention. His rapid and direct style, in refreshing contrast to the laboured classicism of so many of his colleagues, made it hard for reporters to get everything down, and on at least one occasion he was quoted by different newspapers as having expressed himself on opposite sides. Since his speeches were, in any case, often masterpieces of ambiguity, which may or may not have meant the opposite of what they purported to say, an accurate verbatim account would not solve many problems and a close study of the actual record does not get us very far. Nevertheless, it is almost all there is to go on and beyond these ambiguities most things are conjectural.

In 1789 Danton, already thirty, had only five more years to live. The key to the kind of man he was presumably lies in these first thirty years, or would do, if any accurate information survived. Apart from things like his birth certificate and the odd school report, we have not much more than the belated reminiscences of a former school friend and a little material compiled by an admirer some years after Danton's death. To offset this, contemporary evidence is virtually unanimous in presenting Danton as a full-blooded man who enjoyed his pleasures, a good friend who was not too fastidious about the company he kept, and the coiner of phrases that were to drive his biographers into

PREFACE

asterisks. This is all very well as far as it goes, which is not very far: he could still have been either a generous and open-hearted *bon viveur* or a cynical crook. Most of the *bons mots* attributed to him are apocryphal, however closely they correspond to what he is actually known to have said. If the biographer takes all this sort of evidence at its face value he can easily construct an 'Identi-kit' picture which is plausible enough and may well be reasonably accurate. The Danton of legend is hard to resist, especially since he imposed himself on contemporaries as well as posterity. To present him in these terms, however, is merely to endorse a tradition when one ought to be investigating its authenticity. As soon as one tries to do anything of the kind, to eliminate conjecture and start from a basis of verified fact, the whole structure disintegrates. Reduced to 'Danton was a man who – probably – said . . .', we find ourselves back at the starting-point, since we are seldom sure of what he did say and whether or not he meant it.

Danton's actions, paradoxically enough, provide a somewhat surer foothold, despite the fact that he has been labelled as everything from a republican Joan of Arc to a royalist gangster. Unlike many of his colleagues, he saw the Revolution in practical rather than ideal terms. He could speak the language of total revolution and perhaps even carry himself away by his own rhetoric, but he never shared the millenarian views of those intent on creating a new republican man such as the world had never seen. For him, the Revolution was about improving the conditions of men as they were. This still leaves plenty of scope for differences of opinion. Danton was not the kind of man to forget his own interests and his main concern may have been to provide himself and his friends with the means of gratifying their rather expensive tastes. Perhaps he also aspired to create a society in which more would be done for those who could not do very much for themselves. In either case he had both feet firmly planted in the world as he saw it, in which real people actually wanted material things. He saw the Revolution as the means to a political and social end and not as some kind of transcendental god whose priests could aspire to nothing more than martyrdom. Sooner or later it would come to an end and he intended to be on the winning side. Whether he hoped to make a private deal with the Court, rejoiced at the proclamation of a republic or took money from anyone who could be persuaded to part with it, while sacrificing his present paymasters to those he saw as his future allies, are not unimportant questions, but they concern his personal integrity rather than his approach to politics. The essential was to extract as much as possible from what *was* possible, to insure the future for himself, his friends and society at large, to the limited extent that circumstances permitted. This could make him, deservedly, a hero of national defence in the summer of 1792; it could also involve him in less admirable transactions.

My justification for writing another biography of Danton does not lie in any claim to have discovered important new sources of information. I have added one or two scraps to the pile but there is probably not a great deal more for anyone to find. What I have tried to do is to present Danton as a working politician rather than as a stylised figure from one of David's historical paintings. He was the first to sense the scope that the Revolution afforded for mass politics, to appreciate the nature of a political machine and the tactics by which a radical minority could impose itself on an indifferent or hostile electorate. To have grasped all this in 1789 implied talent of a remarkable, if not perhaps a very elevated, order. For better or worse, and on the whole for worse, the machine that Danton created was to play a large part in determining the shape of French politics during the Terror. In that sense at least, his career is inseparable from the history of the Revolution itself. Whether he was a 'genuine' revolutionary or a mere opportunist is the kind of question that he would have been the first to find naïve.

The French Revolution has been the source of so much myth-making that to present Danton in terms considered appropriate to other men in other periods is to invite the accusation of cynicism. Heroes are preferable, villains permissible, but politicians, whatever their virtuosity, have no place in that particular *Gotterdämmerung*. My only defence is to reply that no one finds it odd nowadays that able men should create careers for themselves within a political party of their choice, or even change parties as circumstances alter. Admittedly, they are not often in the pay of the side they claim to be attacking, but if there is any cynicism here it is Danton's rather than mine. The French Revolution was, of course, not entirely the creation of its politicians. It had its mass movements, its visionaries and its fanatics. From the beginning, it existed as symbol and myth, even while its course was being determined by political calculation. The Revolution is far too diverse to be confined within any book, however long. It can only be apprehended if viewed from many angles, often so mutually incompatible as to defy any synthesis. The Mountain of 1793–4, like any other mountain, looks entirely different from different approaches, as the same features change their relationship to each other. The book that follows is no more than a single view from a particular angle. There was no doubt more to Danton than this. There was certainly more to the Revolution than Danton, but rather a lot of it concerned his kind of people and no one has ever found the man himself uninteresting.

Introduction: Danton and the Historians

The French Revolution had scarcely begun before people began writing its history. In the nature of things, contemporaries such as Rabaut Saint-Etienne, Lacretelle and the 'Two Friends of Liberty' could not aspire to more than journalism. After such early efforts France was plunged into the long night of Napoleonic censorship, when the printed word was suspect and the expression of any opinions that departed from official orthodoxy was a crime. It was not until the Restoration that anyone could hope to write – and publish – a serious account of the events that had transformed French government and society. The available sources were still very scanty: newspapers, pamphlets and a growing flood of memoirs and reminiscences, often ghost-written or inflated by enterprising editors from what the veterans thought they could recall (and they recalled a good deal more than they could actually have remembered) from a past that was already a generation old.

The first real historians of the Revolution, Thiers and Mignet, whose accounts appeared in 1823 and 1824, were the prisoners both of their limited sources and of a classical tradition of historical writing. Each aspired to provide an authoritative narrative of how and why things had happened, punctuated by the kind of character studies of the main participants that they had read in Tacitus or Sallust. At least they enjoyed the privileges of the pioneer: they were neither the champions nor the challengers of any particular school and they approached their evidence with a common sense that many of their successors were to lack. Both regarded the Revolution as an inevitable process that was, on the whole, to be welcomed. They identified themselves with none of the revolutionary factions and they considered Danton to have been something of a Catiline, an adventurer of talent, concerned mainly with his own career.

Danton was, according to Mignet,

a gigantic revolutionary; he thought no means blameworthy so long as they were useful and believed that men could do as much as they dared . . . Ardent, overwhelmed with debts and

1

needs, of dissolute habits, devoted to his passions and his party, he was formidable when in pursuit of an objective but became indifferent as soon as he had attained it. A powerful demagogue, he was a mixture of the most opposing vices and qualities. Though he had sold himself to the court, he did not appear sordid . . . He was an absolute exterminator but not personally ferocious . . . He saw revolution as a game in which the victor was free, if he chose, to take the life of the vanquished. In his view, the welfare of his party was superior to the law and even to morality.

Like most of his successors, Mignet found it difficult to maintain a consistent viewpoint when facing the apparent contradictions in Danton's career. He attributed his fall, not to any change of policy, but to his political isolation in 1794; yet he lamented the overthrow of a group that he had described in very unflattering terms: 'Thus perished the last defenders of humanity and moderation.'

Thiers's view of Danton was very similar: 'A failed lawyer, consumed by his passions, he threw himself into the political troubles with ardour and probably in the hope of gain. He was ignorant but endowed with an outstanding intelligence and a vast imagination.' He was a man of extraordinary audacity but without personal hatreds. 'Robespierre was envious, Marat a man of systems, Danton was the passionate man, violent, changeable, cruel and generous in turn . . . full of passions and greedy for glory, he was anything but incorruptible. The court gave him quite considerable sums but only succeeded in paying him, not in buying him.' Like Mignet, Thiers thought Danton the man mainly responsible for the overthrow of the monarchy on 10 August 1792. He believed he had been involved in the prison massacres of the following month and suspected him of intriguing with Dumouriez against the republic. His decline was a product of both his virtues and his vices: he was suspected of corruption and blamed for his reluctance to exterminate fallen enemies. Although he kept in the background in 1794, he was believed to be the leader of those challenging the Committee of Public Safety and was destroyed by his jealous rivals, Robespierre, and Saint-Just.

This picture of Danton as the impetuous and unprincipled revolutionary *par excellence* was taken up by the writers of the period. Julien Sorel, in Stendhal's *Le Rouge et le Noir*, looked up to him as someone who had made his own way in the world, transcending conventional morality in the process: 'The great Danton was a thief'. Balzac, who never accused him of corruption, cited him as typical of the great man whose rise to fame owed nothing to the patient application of the mediocre. 'Don't expect anything great to arise from *self-interest,* because interests change, but expect everything from sentiment, from religious, royalist or patriotic faith. Only these three beliefs produce Richelieus or Dantons.' With the German dramatist, Buchner, who got much of his information from Thiers, the emphasis on feeling became overwhelming. The hero of *Danton's Death* was presented as a world-weary Titan, bored with the Revolution and with life. His fearful lieutenants tried to goad him into action and the little men in office schemed to bring him down. Danton towered above them all, a Byronic figure, cynical, earthy and dissolute, who despised his enemies too much to destroy them by their own ignoble weapons.

The tide was visibly setting towards Romanticism. With Carlyle it reached its flood. Carlyle's *French Revolution* (1837) is more like a series of volcanic explosions than a history. Although he had a shrewd eye for character, he was not much concerned with explaining either the motives of the revolutionaries or the sequence of events. Everything is illuminated by sudden flashes of lightning and then swallowed up in the noise and smoke. Danton emerges for an instant: 'Minister of Justice is his name but Titan of the Forlorn Hope and Enfant Perdu of the Revolution is his quality.' Carlyle does not stop to explain why. Danton reappears briefly, to take his bow. 'He had many sins [Carlyle does not say which] but one worst sin he had not, that of Cant. No hollow Formalist . . . but a real Man.' From now onwards there was to be a good deal of emphasis – which would have pleased Danton – on his masculinity. In those days this was intended as a compliment.

1847 was something of an *annus mirabilis* in the historiography of the Revolution, with the appearance of Lamartine's *Histoire des Girondins* (in fact, a history of the Revolution as a whole, up to 1794) and the first volumes of the histories of Michelet and Louis Blanc. Although contemporary, the three works are very different. Lamartine may have been a Romantic poet but he was a classical historian, the last of the Thiers–Mignet line. Michelet not merely epitomised Romantic history but founded what the Dutch historian, Geyl, has described as the 'revolutionary tradition' which dominated French historical thinking about the Revolution for a century, while Louis Blanc pioneered the social history of the events of 1789–95. Their treatment of Danton was naturally determined by their approach to the revolutionary movement as a whole.

Lamartine carried his classicism to the point of writing accounts of what the revolutionaries *ought* to have said. He invented the speech with which Saint-Just persuaded his colleagues in the governing committees to accept Danton's arrest and elsewhere enlarged on what contemporaries rather implausibly claimed to have remembered saying or hearing, after a lapse of months or years. His sketch of Danton as Catiline was blacker than those of Mignet and Thiers, presenting him as the prototype of the Mafia boss. As he disarmingly admitted in a private letter, 'I accuse Danton without proof, out of the honest need to find a criminal in order to personify the horror that crime inspires.'

> Devoid of honour, principles or morality, he liked democracy only for its excitement . . . He worshipped force and force alone. His genius lay solely in his contempt for honesty and he thought himself superior to everyone else since he had trampled all scruples underfoot. Everything was means to him. He was a statesman of materialism . . . Such a man is bound to be profoundly indifferent to both despotism and liberty. His contempt for the people must incline him towards the side of tyranny . . . The court was well aware of the price of his conscience. He threatened it so that it would want to buy him; he only opened his mouth to have it stuffed with gold. His most revolutionary movements merely marked up the price at which he could be bought . . . He *was* bought every day and next morning was up for sale again . . . He was the focus of all those looking for nothing but fortune and impunity. But whereas others had only the baseness of crime, Danton's vices reached heroic proportions and his intellect amounted almost to genius.

That must have made Lamartine feel uncommonly virtuous. However, he found it just as hard as everyone else to be consistent. Like a true Romantic, he warmed to his subject as Danton began to fail. 'Tired of being terrible, he wanted to be loved . . . Danton was a man, Robespierre was an idea.' He thought Danton, at his trial, displayed 'more pride than innocence', but nevertheless asserted, with a fine disregard for the evidence, that none of the jurors believed him to be guilty. His final summing-up was rather more generous than his earlier indictment. 'His only deficiency as a great man was virtue . . . He had low vices but generous passions.' Since Lamartine wrote history in terms of what ought to have been, Danton, at the end of his life, was appropriately overcome by remorse for his past misdeeds.

For Michelet, the Revolution was an epic of the French people as a whole. Like Tolstoy, he saw individual leaders as symbols rather than as makers of history. The French Revolution, however, was much more than a tragic pageant. It was the decisive turning-point in the history of civilisation, the beginning of the post-Christian era, a new gospel and a message of redemption to the nations that only the French people could have proclaimed. In an ironical but presumably unconscious imitation of the New Testament, Michelet presented revolutionary France as crucified by a Europe that it came to save. It was all of a piece and it was essentially good. Whatever might seem reprehensible – the September massacres or the Terror – was forced upon it by the ferocity of its pharisaical persecutors. Henceforth this comforting doctrine was to become the root of orthodoxy. Liberal or socialist scions could be grafted on to it at will, but the vigour of the plants derived from Michelet's stock.

Since Michelet's commitment was to the revolutionary tide rather than to those who swam in it, Danton's credit rose and fell to the extent that he seemed to be identified with the movement as a whole. As Michelet approached the summer of 1792, when the monarchy was overthrown and France, under Danton's leadership, defied the Austrian and Prussian invaders, Danton became the incarnation of the Revolution, 'perhaps its strongest and most penetrating genius'.

Danton was great-hearted. This prodigious orator, both instinctive and calculating, had as his basis in the people's affection a powerful and sensual temperament, altogether designed for physical love, dominated by flesh and blood. Danton was firstly and above everything else a male . . . Beneath his violent and furious mask one could also feel the presence of a heart . . .

The tragic name of Danton, however soiled and disfigured it may be, either by himself or by the parties, will still remain at the bottom of the dear memories and regrets of France.

He was also, and this idea was to have a rich future, the only revolutionary orator not to draw his inspiration from Rousseau. Michelet at first denied any similarity between Danton and Diderot. 'Danton is vigorous and positive, Diderot windy and vague.' Later on he altered this verdict – of Diderot rather than of Danton – describing the revolutionary as the true son of the *philosophe*.

In 1793–4, when Danton failed to unite the republicans and the fierce current of the Revolution swept him to one side, Michelet had to abandon him too. With the morality of a Saint–Just, he pronounced that Danton was 'not pure enough to hate evil'. As Michelet saw it, his independent career was over by the summer of 1793. Henceforth he was increasingly *robespierrisé* and by 1794 he had become 'the most lamentable of all the ruins'. Towards the end of his life he was concerned merely with self-preservation, turning against his own supporters in the hope of appeasing Robespierre. Although Michelet was scathing about the parody of a trial to which Danton was subjected, he subscribed to Buchner's world-weary thesis and thought his former hero relieved to be rid of an impossible rôle. Like Lamartine, though for different reasons and in the opposite direction, Michelet's judgment of Danton turned full circle between 1792 and 1794.

Both Michelet and Louis Blanc brought a new depth to the historiography of the French Revolution. Though they did not quote their sources they based their writing on a much deeper scrutiny of the records than their predecessors had thought necessary. Louis Blanc, perhaps because of his experience as a minister of the Second Republic in 1848, showed a remarkable grasp of the party politics of 1793–4, combining shrewd psychological insight with a sharp eye for tactics and admirable detachment. He agreed with Lamartine's antithesis between Danton the man of action and Robespierre the personified idea, but attributed the defeat of the former to the fact that the Revolution was 'essentially an idea, a principle'. Intellectually and ideologically, Blanc's sympathies were with Robespierre, but he admitted that the passion and complexity of Danton made him the more attractive character. He described him as 'the statesman of chaos', believed him responsible for 'the most murderous measures, but half absolved by the involuntary sympathy he inspires . . . His apparent fury was often a kind of generous hypocrisy . . . He gave himself the airs of a barbarian to win the power to be humane'. Louis Blanc was another admirer of Danton's 'masculine simplicity'. In his careful reconstruction of the political feuds of the Jacobins in the winter of 1793–4 he presented Danton as the active ally of Robespierre and not as a member of the group – which most historians have described as 'Dantonist' – that attacked the Committee of Public Safety. He thought that Danton, perhaps from lassitude, retired into the background, but that the governing committees suspected him of being the secret leader of the opposition. He condemned Robespierre's 'reprehensible weakness' in agreeing to Danton's proscription on grounds of suspicion alone.

Despite their different viewpoints, the historians of 1847, Lamartine, Michelet and Louis Blanc, had some things in common. Their concern was with the Revolution as a whole and their assessment of Danton was determined by this general perspective. All three thought that things went wrong in 1793–4 and either condemned Danton (Michelet) for failing to prevent this, or sympathised with him (Lamartine and Louis Blanc) for becoming the victim of forces outside his control. Although they tended to present him as essentially masculine, and equated masculinity with action as opposed to ideology, they were all aware that he did not fit easily into any preconceived pattern. The man of feeling, the plaything of his emotions, was also a shrewd and calculating politician. When they stressed that he was above all a man, they implied nothing more and nothing less. None of them was tempted to bill him as Superman.

A different group – some of them blasted by Michelet as 'catholico-robespierrists' – refused to worship at the altar of masculinity. There was a Robespierrist tradition that went back to the days of the Incorruptible himself. Buonarroti, who had been a member of Robespierre's circle, kept his memory alive into the 1820s. Sympathetic interpretations by Laponneraye (1838), Tissot (*Histoire de Robespierre*, 1844) and Cabet (1845) prolonged this to the eve of the 1848 revolution. Buonarroti was perhaps mainly responsible for the rather implausible view of Robespierre as a social rather than a political revolutionary. A different branch of the Robespierrist tradition, weightily supported by Buchez, whose forty-volume *Histoire parlementaire de la Révolution française* began to appear in 1834, put the emphasis on Robespierre as the prophet of the spiritual transformation of man and society. The Robespierrists agreed with Lamartine and Louis Blanc that their hero was a personified idea, and for the time being he was the only revolutionary to be acclaimed as the standard-bearer of an ideology. This was soon to change and the conception of Danton too was to take on new and bizarre dimensions.

When Auguste Comte, the founder of positivism, touched on the French Revolution in his lectures of 1839–42 he paid no particular attention to Danton. He seems to have been subsequently impressed by the history of the Revolution published by Villiaumé in 1850, the first to deny Danton's corruption, and he may have been struck by Michelet's description of Danton as the heir of Diderot. When Comte published his *Système de Politique Positive* in 1851–4, Danton emerged in a new and unexpected light as the prophet of positivism. For Comte, there had been three tendencies within the French Enlightenment of the eighteenth century, the negative rationalism of Voltaire, the religiosity of Rousseau and Diderot's prefiguration of positivism. Each of these three attitudes had inspired a political faction during the Revolution: the Girondins, Robespierre and Danton. Whereas the revolutionaries in general were misled into a blind devotion to parliamentary institutions for their own sake,

Danton and his followers, who represented the school of Diderot, were superior to these demagogic illusions . . . Their ascendancy of ten months, intervening between the indispensable expulsion of the talkers [the Girondins] and the bloody triumph of the fanatics [Robespierre] is a period which, in the final judgment of history, will always represent the one French Assembly that deserves to be remembered. The real need was to establish the true religion, to discover, in both public and private life, a single centre round which men can concentrate their feelings, their thoughts and their actions. This need had been worthily understood by Danton and his representatives alone . . . When Danton succumbed to the sullen jealousy of a bloody pontificator, the new dictatorship degenerated into a reactionary anarchy that will always remain without a parallel.

This was enough for the eager band of Comte's disciples who galloped away with the bit between their teeth. Danton had now become, not so much a cause as *the* Cause.

The contribution of the positivists to the history of the Revolution was not wholly mischievous. Their concept of a science of humanity, reinforced by the example of German historical scholarship, brought a new seriousness to the writing of history. From now onwards historians produced their documents and cited their references. Like Michelet's invention of the revolutionary tradition, this new belief in scientific history was to be a lasting acquisition. The most recent historiographer of the French Revolution, Jacques Godechot, in *Un Jury pour la Révolution* (1974) calls his last chapter, 'Towards a more scientific history'. One may remain sceptical about a 'science' whose practitioners get no closer to any kind of consensus and whose interpretation of what they choose to select as relevant evidence corresponds so demonstrably to the political and ideological opinions with which they started, but at least the recognition of the need to produce the evidence is some sort of gain.

The positivists were helped by the appearance in 1861 of Bougeart's *Danton, Documents authentiques pour servir à l'histoire de la Révolution française*, whose title significantly put Danton before the Revolution. In his introduction, Bougeart wrote, 'What recommends this work to the public is its impartiality', a new emphasis that would not have seemed necessary or appropriate to earlier historians. It is the first biography of Danton, it is well documented . . . and it is also entirely eulogistic. Bougeart saved his trump cards for his conclusion: a letter from Danton's two sons and a memoir of 1791 which he believed confirmed Villiaumé's assertion that Danton had not been corrupt.

Inspired by Comte and fortified by Bougeart, Dr Robinet took the field to prove that Danton was not so much the greatest leader of the Revolution as the *only* one to understand its significance and its pivotal rôle in the advance of civilisation. In the preface to his first book, *Le Procès des Dantonists* (1879), which included Villiaumé among its numerous dedications, Robinet put his cards on the table. 'The appreciation of the French Revolution occupies an inevitably restricted space . . . in the philosophy of Auguste Comte. He therefore expressed the hope that one of his disciples would write a short history of the Revolution from the viewpoint of his doctrine.' After a modest disclaimer of his qualifications for such a task, Robinet did his best. At least he knew what was expected of him and he left his readers in no doubt about where he stood. Danton's death was 'an odious crime, since its victims were irreproachable patriots, its end was iniquitous and its means execrable; it was a fatal crime since it destroyed men indispensable to the republic, so that the bloodthirsty and incompetent could have their brief hour of triumph, and it inflicted on the normal development of civilisation a deviation from which we are still suffering today . . . It is the reversal of this verdict that we have come to demand of public opinion.'

Danton, Mémoire sur sa vie privée (1884), this time dedicated to the memory of Bougeart, gave Robinet a chance to celebrate the paladin's domestic virtues: 'An excellent son, a good father and husband, a benevolent master, devoted to his friends and compatriots, a citizen of integrity wholly devoted to the public good, in which respect he could serve as a model to so many of those who have treated him so shamefully.' The most Robinet would concede in the way of criticism was that Danton, under extreme provocation, used rather strong language. 'Danton, in fact, gave himself to the Revolution and to his country with total self-abnegation, for them and not for himself, with no thought of personal advantage or ambition. He was so free from personal ambition that his excessive lack of concern for himself, combined with his disinterestedness and generosity, prevented him from taking and keeping the government as the consolidation of the Revolution required.' He was, in other words, too good for this world and certainly much too good to be true.

Danton, émigré (1887) was a rather disappointing collection of scraps, but the centenary of the Revolution in 1889 and the campaign to provide Danton with a statue (in the end he got two, one in Paris and one in his birthplace at Arcis-sur-Aube) found Robinet back in fighting form, with *Danton, Homme d'état*. Comte received due credit for inspiring others to 'evaluate in detail the range, the rectitude and the superiority of [Danton's] political actions and also his integrity and personal morality'. All that was left now was for someone to equate him with Joan of Arc. This gap was promptly filled by Antoine – described by Robinet as another disciple of Comte – when he unveiled the statue at Arcis, an occasion that perhaps excused a certain amount of hyperbole. 'To the intellectual freedom of the Athenian, to Spartan integrity and Roman grandeur, Danton allied the most generous sentiments of human nature [besides serving as a one-man compendium of European history]. Like Joan of Arc, he carried within himself an inexhaustible love for the labouring masses, whose dignity, consolation and happiness was the goal of his activity.' Danton's own comment on that would probably have been most unsuitable for the ears of the Maid of Orleans. He would no doubt have concluded too that, after such an apotheosis, there was nowhere to go but down.

After quoting Antoine and others, Robinet elevated the discussion to a more philosophical plane. 'We should like ourselves to enlarge on these precious but too concise texts. [Danton] had a feeling for the elevated goal to which the evolution of human civilisation was tending and wanted to assure, by spiritual liberty and public order, the transitional régime and temporary shelter that would enable science to complete the elaboration and propagation of the theoretical basis for the regeneration of the west.' He had to concede that Danton had made one serious mistake : when he combined with Robespierre in an attempt to halt the attack on Christianity, towards the end of 1793. However regrettable, this was understandable, since Comte had not yet established the theoretical basis of positivism, and Danton, for all his genius, had only an intuitive glimpse of the Promised Land. It all sounds very familiar and subsequent self-appointed friends of the 'labouring masses' were to excuse the mistakes of Saint-Just and Babeuf on the ground that they could not have read Marx. Lenin, who was more fortunately placed, did see himself as inaugurating a 'transitional régime' in that regeneration of the west that is taking such an unconscionable time.

Like all proper religions, positivism had its heretics. Taine, whose *Origines de la France contemporaine* began to appear in 1875, used the positivist technique of going to the primary sources as the basis for his root-and-branch condemnation of the Revolution as a betrayal of the true spirit of French history by mean and envious men thinking only of their own advancement. Danton, 'a second-rate lawyer from a hovel in Champagne', could quite easily be fitted into the new scenario. Taine admitted that he showed himself to be a real leader in the summer of 1792, but his methods were those of the successful brigand and his authority rested on his lavish distribution of the spoils.

> Glutted in this way, the pack of starving 'brawlers' and the insatiable 'intriguers', all the activists of Sections and clubs are in his hands . . . He combines the temperament of a butcher with the heart of a man . . . the outbursts of a *clubiste* with the lucidity of a politician; he is not the dupe of his own bombastic language and he knows the price of the rogues he employs . . . There is a close similarity between the demagogue and the brigand: both are gang leaders.

If Taine magnified Danton's share in the Revolution, it was merely to emphasise his villainy. 'Despotism founded on conquest and maintained by fear, the despotism of the Jacobin and Parisian plebs, that was his aim and those were his means.' This was an even blacker portrait than Lamartine's since Taine admitted of no extenuating circumstances at all. The positivist historians, between them, had covered the extremes of adulation and abuse. It was an odd product of the new 'scientific' history.

In 1891 Alphonse Aulard became the first occupant of the new chair in French revolutionary history at the Sorbonne. From now onwards the specialised study of the Revolution came to be concentrated mainly in the universities, with the gentleman amateur content to digest the findings of the professionals into elegant prose. The professionalisation of history was a mixed blessing. It brought a far higher standard of erudition and a quite remarkable familiarity with massive quantities of evidence. With this went an increasingly critical attitude to sources, a painful awareness of the fragility of so much that had passed for evidence and a recognition of the need to substantiate judgements instead of merely advancing them. It could also involve a certain loss of nerve, a tendency to leave the documents to point their own conclusions and a suspicion of historical imagination. Men who were hot for certainties often came up with dusty answers. Aulard's last article on Danton, published in 1922, concluded that *all* the evidence for his much-quoted sayings at the end of his life was inconclusive. 'It is probable that he said them. One hopes that he said them. Historically speaking, one cannot be sure. Perhaps they are more true than authentic.' Aulard's dilemma is that of all his successors. If history is to be truly scientific it has nothing to say that is worth hearing. If it tries to fulfil the rôle that once gave it importance, that of interpreting the past to the present, much of what it presents as true will be only conjectural at best and at times wrong.

Aulard was well disposed towards Danton but far too level-headed a historian to accept him in the pantomime rôle of Fairy Queen for which most of the positivists had cast him. He published a fierce attack on Taine in 1907 and long before this he had produced a favourable series of articles on Danton, most of them appearing in the review that he founded, *La Révolution française*. These are still the starting-point for any serious study of Danton today. Although Danton was Aulard's hero, his respect for his subject stayed well on this side of idolatry. After an early article claiming once again to refute the charges of corruption, Aulard went on to study Danton as an exponent of *realpolitik* on the first Committee of Public Safety, trying to negotiate peace with England and Prussia and to isolate Austria. In 'Auguste Comte and the French Revolution', which appeared in 1892, he endorsed much of the positivists' praise of Danton, but not for their reasons. Danton, he insisted, was not the only saint, but 'the most modern statesman of the Revolution, with a mind turned towards the future, a practical politician, an eloquent orator, but a man of weak character and lazy'. Robinet could not be expected to stand for that. He broke with Aulard and attacked him in an anonymous pamphlet which, of course, everyone identified. Undeterred, Aulard went on to publish in the following year a number of biographical articles tracing Danton's career from his youth to the end of 1793. The intention was to justify him, but the tone was quiet and expository. In his *Histoire politique de la Révolution française* (1901) he presented the Revolution, somewhat in the manner of Michelet, as a collective movement whose leaders derived their influence and importance from the forces behind them. He went so far as to deny that they were 'a generation of giants' and suggested that the orators of his own day were the equals of Danton and Robespierre. This was demystification with a vengeance, to the point of challenging the revolutionary tradition itself. It looked as though Danton, for all the merits that Aulard recognised in him, would fade into the *grisaille* to which 'scientific' history reduced those whom a previous generation had acclaimed as geniuses.

Danton was saved from such routine celebrity by Aulard's most

talented pupil, Mathiez. According to his own account, Mathiez was brought up in the Dantonist orthodoxy. 'I had been nourished by the legend. I believed in the generous Danton, treacherously assassinated by the ambitious Robespierre.' About 1908 he suddenly and dramatically broke with Aulard – and with Danton. Whether his condemnation of Danton was the cause or the consequence of his breach with Aulard is not clear. Mathiez himself claimed that it was his research into the religious history of the Revolution that led him to suspect the motives of those attacking Christianity towards the end of 1793. This is a very peculiar explanation since it was precisely Danton's association with Robespierre in opposition to the dechristianisers that Robinet had considered his only political mistake. It is true that people who may have been Danton's political allies were active opponents of the Catholic Church and one of Mathiez's more questionable practices was to classify as 'Dantonist' anyone who at any time voted with Danton, criticised his opponents or was put on trial with him. Whatever the actual reason for Mathiez's change of front, it was probably connected with the politics of the Third Republic. Both he and Aulard were men of the Left, but whereas the older man was a Radical who wrote for the great Radical newspaper, *La Dépêche de Toulouse,* Mathiez was inclined towards socialism and occasionally contributed to *Humanité,* though he was to denounce the Stalinist régime towards the end of his life. After being press-ganged by the positivists into the service of their philosophy, Danton now found himself forced to sail under the political colours of the Third Republic. Mathiez could see the dangers of this approach to history clearly enough when it was done by someone else. He said in one of his lectures, 'Aulard is not a historian. He transposes the present into the past and presents the Jacobins as though they were Radicals. It is ridiculous.' He was presumably less aware that he behaved in exactly the same way. When the socialists condemned the links between politics and finance, he attacked the 'Dantonists' as crooked speculators. When nationalistic Frenchmen denounced the attempts at a negotiated peace in 1916, Mathiez attacked Danton as a defeatist and when the country became alarmed at the real or imaginary activities of foreign spies and their French agents, he wrote *La Révolution et les étrangers* in 1918.
One thing remained constant: whatever the enemy of the mo-

ment, Danton had stood for the same sort of thing during the Revolution. 'Everywhere I kept coming across the name of Danton.' Mathiez at first regarded the revolutionary leader as no worse than venal, but he eventually convinced himself that he was a traitor as well. Danton, whom the positivists had elevated to the position that Lenin was to occupy in Stalinist historiography, now became a Trotsky, a counter-revolutionary British agent and 'a real bandit whom a stupid legend has passed off as a hero'.

He was a crooked and sceptical politician, quick to despair of the success of the Revolution, an unscrupulous intriguer whose secret actions were the exact opposite of his public declarations, a common rake trying to turn war-weariness to the advantage of his own base ambition and patch up a shameful peace at any price, the indulgent chief of all the defeatists of the time.

Mathiez brought to the service of his monomania inexhaustible energy and unrivalled erudition. He discovered a great deal of new evidence about the history of the Revolution and the scores of articles he published, many of them collected into half a dozen books, are often models of detective work. He made it impossible for anyone to look at Danton in the old way, but he handled his evidence like a prosecutor rather than a judge. Everything was interpreted to Danton's discredit and when Danton supported Mathiez's hero, Robespierre, it was always for the wrong reasons. The reliability of sources depended on the extent to which they said what Mathiez believed and he would accept against Danton the kind of evidence that would merely have proved the unreliability of the witness if directed against Robespierre. Danton could do nothing right. Mathiez conceded that he was not directly responsible for the September massacres, but this was only because he 'despised human life too much to be bloodthirsty'. Fouquier-Tinville, the prosecutor of the revolutionary tribunal, would not have disowned that one. This is not to deny that much of what Mathiez wrote against Danton was true, but the implications of his discoveries may not always have been what he said they were.

In the year of Mathiez's death, 1932, Georges Lefebvre, who was to succeed him in Aulard's old chair at the Sorbonne, published in the review that Mathiez had founded, the *Annales historiques de la Révolution française,* a long article in which he tried to arrive at a general assessment of Danton's career. This was obviously intended as a corrective to Mathiez's demonology. Admirably dispassionate and concerned to understand Danton as he was, rather than to enlist him in the service of any particular cause, it is still the best assessment of Danton's place in the Revolution. Lefebvre occupied the middle ground: Danton was corrupt, but he was also a good patriot. He rendered great services to France and to the Revolution in the summer of 1792, but his subsequent diplomacy pursued unattainable objectives and his attempt to stop the Terror before victory had been won was irresponsible. Lefebvre was perhaps less convincing when he tried to reconcile in a single synthesis the conflicting views of Danton as the slave of his own impulses and the crafty and calculating politician. He thought that Danton tried to manipulate his audience but could not have succeeded as he did if he had not also succumbed to its influence. As Lefebvre was the first to admit, a good deal still remained obscure and enigmatic.

Since 1932 the question of Danton has remained where Lefebvre left it. Occasional biographies have continued to appear, the best of them being Hérissay's *Cet excellent M. Danton* (1960), but without significant additions to the evidence or its interpretation. Perhaps one should make an exception of Guérin's *La lutte des classes sous la première république*, which was intended as a Trotskyite interpretation of the Revolution, presenting it as a succession of class conflicts, with the 'leaders' little more than labels for the conflicting social forces. Guérin challenged the 'orthodox' view of Robespierre, presenting both him and Danton as spokesmen for a 'revolutionary bourgeoisie' that was impatient to shake off its dependence on its sansculotte allies and bring the revolution to an end. Faced with the difficult problem of explaining why, in this case, the one should have connived at the death of the other, Guérin fell back on the traditional explanations: Robespierre's jealousy and Danton's impatience.

Danton's place in the mythology of the Revolution is clear enough. His position in its history remains ambiguous. Lefebvre's estimate of his political importance may well prove acceptable to future generations but there is more to it than that. It would be rash to prophesy that he will never again be taken up as a symbol when a new generation discovers what the Revolution was 'really' about. His character and motives, despite all that has been written

16

about him, remain enigmatic. Guérin put it very well when he said that 'Danton obscures and confuses everything he touches'. This was generally because he intended to. There is still room for conjecture and, barring the unlikely discovery of a great deal of new evidence about a man who was careful to cover his tracks, the argument can go on indefinitely. If the story of Danton's fate at the hands of the historians proves anything at all, it shows that what people make of him reflects their preoccupations in the present as much as the evidence of the past.

I The Beginning of a Career

Georges-Jacques Danton was born on 26 October 1759 in Arcis-sur-Aube, which was not much more than a village in Champagne. He shared with most of the future revolutionaries his age, his provincial origins and a comfortable middle-class family background. His grandfather had been a farmer but his father had moved a little way up the social ladder and held a minor legal office in Arcis. There were Dantons all over the neighbourhood and one of Georges-Jacques's more successful uncles was a canon at nearby Troyes. Danton himself was one of a family of ten. His father, who had been twice married, died quite young, when Georges-Jacques was only three, and his mother remarried when he was eleven. These could have been disturbing experiences, as family disasters seem to have been for his contemporary, Robespierre, but there is no evidence that they were. Cushioned by the reassuring presence of so many other Dantons, Georges-Jacques seems to have taken life as it came. He had a gift for getting on with people and throughout his life his relationship with his own and his wife's families was affectionate and untroubled.

Virtually nothing is known for certain about his childhood. The only evidence comes from the reminiscences of his school-mate, Béon, written down long after Danton's death, and from what was collected at second hand by one of his protégés, Rousselin de Saint-Albin, who first met Danton during the Revolution.[1] Both present him as a vigorous extrovert, unperturbed by his encounters with the local fauna. He is said to have been gored by a jealous bull when he himself was being suckled by a cow, which gave him a permanently disfigured lip. His flattened nose was a memento from another bull and he also got himself trampled by a herd of pigs. While he was still a boy he was badly marked by smallpox. If there is any factual basis for these bucolic misfortunes, they seem to have left him with a face of rather less than classical proportions and an understandable conviction of his indestructibility.

1. The best account is in A. Aulard, 'L'enfance et la jeunesse de Danton', in his *Etudes et leçons sur la Révolution française*, 4th series, Paris, 1908.

After beginning his education at the local school, he was sent on to Troyes, where he lodged in the town and was spared the rigours of boarding-school discipline. The college at Troyes was maintained by the Oratorian Order, which put more emphasis on science, history and modern languages than was customary in eighteenth-century France. Danton probably responded to this and found life congenial enough. The college records show that he won the occasional prize and he occupied an honourable, if undistinguished position, *inter bonos,* along with his future chronicler, Béon, and Paré, who was to follow him throughout the revolution. A plausible story, told by Rousselin, maintains that in 1775 he escaped from the college and made his way on foot to Reims to watch the coronation of the new king, Louis XVI, who, by an odd coincidence, was to be treated on his return to Paris to a Latin oration from the schoolboy Robespierre. The Oratorians apparently took an indulgent view of the escapade even if they did not, in fact, give Danton a prize for his account of the coronation.

Danton was to be one of the few revolutionaries who did not regard himself as a latter-day Roman. His uniquely blunt speeches owed very little to classical models and imagery, and the classical texts in his library were all in French, English or Italian translations. He could both read and speak English and he had a reading knowledge of Italian. If one compares him with his contemporaries it is easy, especially for the academic, to get the impression that he was the kind of self-made man who advertises his contempt for book-learning. His critics have sometimes called him uneducated. This probably means little more than that he expressed himself in everyday language and was not forever adjusting an imaginary toga. The admiring Rousselin claimed that Danton was familiar with the works of Montesquieu, Voltaire, Rousseau, Beccaria and especially Buffon; he even maintained that his hero memorised the *Encyclopaedia*, which is carrying things a little far. Danton certainly had all these authors in his library in 1793.[2] His collection then included few classical authors and virtually nothing on the law, but a wide range of books of the Enlightenment: 91 volumes of Voltaire, 58 of Buffon, 16 of Rousseau, most of the *Encyclopaedia* and various works by Raynal,

2. The inventory is in Robinet, *Danton émigré*, Paris, 1887, pp. 268–71.

Mably and Helvétius. Besides the few Italian books, there was a substantial English section: Adam Smith's *Wealth of Nations, The Spectator*, Pope, Johnson's dictionary, Blackstone, Robertson's histories of Scotland and America and even eight volumes of 'Schakespeare', who at the time had few readers in France. Danton may not have been an intellectual but the evidence suggests that he was a cultured man, and his culture presumably rested on the foundations laid by the Oratorians.

As his studies came to an end the family began to think about a career for him. Like most of his contemporaries, he found the law more appealing than the church, and like many of the future revolutionaries he decided to chance his luck in Paris, where he went at twenty-one, to become a lawyer's clerk. Before setting off he made over to his step-father all his claims on his dead father's estate. This was no more than a fair return for all the money spent on his education, but it suggests harmonious family relations and speaks well for Danton's generosity. When his Parisian employer objected to his execrable handwriting, Danton is said to have replied that he was not looking for a job as a copyist. To make any progress in his profession he needed a law degree. Fortunately these were easily obtained, at a reasonable price and without any fuss about the need for years of study, from the university of Reims. Danton graduated about 1784 – which entitled him to join the long queue of brief-hunting lawyers, with whom Paris was over-supplied.

By the late 1780s Danton's career – and he was already approaching thirty – corresponded to a familiar pattern in late eighteenth-century France: a good education, legal qualifications, the Parisian gamble and impecunious obscurity. He was original only in the fact that he did not see himself as a future *philosophe,* for there is no evidence that he ever had any literary ambitions. Paris was full of such people, living from hand to mouth and gradually forced into hack writing for their social superiors, to pornography, to anything that might save them from a return, defeated, to the sleepy provincial towns they had left with such high hopes. Whatever their talents, they found reputation and respectability hard to come by in a legal and literary world where the established had barred the doors against the vociferous crowd of outsiders. In default of the literary triumph to which most of them aspired, the only chance of a break-through, of crossing the vital frontier that separated the successful from those who were merely qualified, was the purchase of a legal office, and this was beyond the means of almost all of them. It was no wonder that they welcomed the revolutionary crisis of 1789 as a gift from Providence. Danton, however, had made his own arrangements.

In appropriate circumstances, marriage was one of the few ways of raising capital in eighteenth-century France, but it normally required birth, influence or office to trade against a substantial dowry. Danton had not much to offer in any of these respects and he could scarcely hope that the rules of the social game would be waived in favour of his good looks. He may well have impressed women by his masculinity, his energy, and qualities important in life that slip through the wide mesh of historical records. We shall never know what Antoinette-Gabrielle Charpentier saw in him or why her father, who supplemented a small income from his employment with the national tax farm by keeping a café that was popular with lawyers, allowed her to marry him. He must have looked a risky investment, his superior social status, such as it was, offset by the need to launch him on a career. Whatever the feelings of the parties may have been – and perhaps they were all more concerned with love than with money – Danton's marriage provided him with an escape route into respectability.

Like all his financial transactions, his purchase of the office of *avocat aux Conseils du Roi* was somewhat peculiar.[3] It was sold to him by Huet de Paisy, in March 1787, for 78,000 livres (about £3,500 in eighteenth-century terms). Danton had to find 56,000 at once, another 10,000 as soon as he was formally accepted by his future colleagues and the remainder within four years. He put down 5,000 himself and borrowed 15,000 from his future father-in-law, Charpentier. The remaining 36,000 were lent to him by a Mlle Duhauttoir, who came from Troyes and may have been known to him. She was certainly known to Huet and was, in fact, his mistress. It was perhaps no more than a coincidence that the notary who transacted the business should have been succeeded a little later by one of Danton's brothers-in-law. All this may simply mean that the Dantons liked to keep their business affairs within the circle of their family and friends, but the transaction was

3. G. Pioro, 'Sur la fortune de Danton', *Annales historiques de la Révolution française*, 1955.

peculiar in other ways. Huet himself had bought the office in 1774 for a mere 30,000 livres, which he had never paid. This suggests that Danton paid an absurdly inflated price for it. On the other hand, the faithful Rousselin said it brought in an annual income of 20–25,000 livres, which implies that Huet virtually gave it away. Rousselin, of course, may have invented his figure to provide a respectable explanation of Danton's relative affluence during the early years of the Revolution. One could only reconcile these apparent contradictions if, as seemed natural to the more admiring of Danton's biographers, he infused new life into a moribund practice. It seems a big 'if'.

Whatever the bald facts conceal, and if anything was concealed it is unlikely to emerge now, Danton's position was transformed by his new office. The *avocats aux Conseils du Roi* were a respected body of lawyers who presented cases before the royal councils and their delegated commissions. The office conferred special social status because of this close association with the court at Versailles and it was about this time that Georges-Jacques began signing himself 'd'Anton', a style he was to retain until both he and 'de Robespierre' reverted to their baptismal names in 1792.

There is no means of knowing how hard Danton worked and if he really did earn more than 20,000 livres a year. The twenty-two cases in which he is known to have been involved, over a period of about four years, may be only a fraction of the total. For a future revolutionary, some of them had a certain irony: in 1787 he appeared for two men trying to prove their noble ancestry, and in January 1789 he defended a seigneur who was attempting to enclose common land. Perhaps this does not matter; lawyers plead the cases of those who pay them. More important is the fact that Danton was involved in the world that gravitated round Versailles. Unlike most of the future revolutionaries, he was connected with the king's councils and not with the appeal courts, or Parlements, where most of the country's eminent lawyers were conducting a noisy campaign against what they liked to describe as 'ministerial despotism'. One of Danton's earliest cases was the defence of Barentin in a civil suit. Barentin was already the head of an important court, the *Cour des Aides,* and he was to become Minister of Justice in 1788. Robinet claimed that he was so impressed by a programme of political reform submitted to him by

Danton that he twice offered to make Danton secretary of the Chancellery. This is improbable, and Robinet's date – August 1787 – is certainly wrong since Barentin did not become minister for another year. Rousselin said that Danton also got to know the Brienne brothers, one of whom was Minister of Finance and virtually Prime Minister from the spring of 1787 to the summer of 1788. Even if these are pious exaggerations, he would certainly have had the opportunity to make useful contacts at court and he was a man who knew how to cultivate relationships of this kind.

Rousselin also said that when Danton was called upon to make the newcomer's customary impromptu Latin address to his colleagues, the subject chosen for him was 'the moral and political state of the country in its relationship to justice'. Danton startled his fellow-lawyers with a powerful exposition of the dangers of the situation and called for a royal policy of reform that would impose sacrifices on the clergy and the nobility, warning his audience that the 'constitutional' opposition of the Paris Parlement was no more than a screen for the protection of its own interests. At one point he allegedly thundered, 'Woe betide those who provoke revolutions! Woe betide those who make them!' If this incident rests on any basis of fact it suggests, not that Danton was already an opponent of the régime, but that he was giving dramatic form to the ministerial point of view, when most of the French legal profession were aligned with the Parlements in opposition to the court. There would be nothing surprising in this. Danton was no doubt anxious to get off to a good start and both conviction and self-interest might well suggest that the future lay with reforming ministers who were making cautious overtures to the mass of the population in order to outflank the opposition of the upper clergy and the nobility.

As soon as Danton had bought his office he married Gabrielle Charpentier, on 9 June 1787. She brought him a dowry of 18,000 livres, together with another 2,000 of her own savings. Most of this presumably paid off the 15,000 livres which her father had advanced to Danton for purchase of his office. He began his married life in a small flat in the rue des Mauvaises Paroles, but within a year the couple moved to the rue des Cordeliers, near to the Luxembourg, where he was to spend the rest of his life. He rented a substantial apartment, with two salons, a dining-room and three bedrooms.[4] The neighbourhood was not particularly fashionable, but the rent must have been higher than one would have expected a man as heavily in debt as Danton to be able to afford. He may have felt that his new dignity called for an appropriate setting and that the best way to become a well-established lawyer was to behave as though he was one already.

By 1789 it looked as though he had settled down. He had certainly come a long way from the farmyards of Arcis, even if his financial situation showed more promise than performance. His future political enemy, Madame Roland – not the most reliable of witnesses – wrote four years later that, at the beginning of the Revolution, he had more debts than briefs. According to Madame Roland, Gabrielle admitted that the household had depended on regular subsidies from Charpentier. In spite of all that, as long as his luck lasted, Danton was doing well. He had an attractive wife and although his first son, born in 1788, was to die in April 1789, two others were to follow. He had a spacious apartment which an inventory of February 1793 showed to be well stocked with furniture and household effects valued at 9,000 livres. No doubt some of these were acquired during the Revolution, but his marriage contract already contained a reference to his library. He had an office of some importance that might serve as a jumping-off ground for eventual ennoblement. He had no doubt picked up useful contacts at Versailles and was well established in Paris where he had friends in the neighbourhood among the habitués of the café Procope. He had certainly done much better than most: Paré, his old school friend and a man four years his senior, was his chief clerk. Deforgues also worked in his office and a man called Billaud-Varenne helped him from time to time. Four years later Paré was to be Minister of the Interior, Deforgues Foreign Secretary and Billaud-Varenne a member of the Committee of Public Safety, but in 1789 Danton was their employer. Of all the Brissots, Desmoulins and the crowd of those who had gambled on Paris, he was one of the very few to have brought it off. Unlike the rest of them, he did not need a revolution, and if one came, he was free to choose his side.

4. There is a sketch of the apartment in J. Hérissay, *Cet excellent M. Danton*, Paris, 1960, p. 40.

II The Creation of a Machine

The year 1789 was one of the most dramatic in the whole turbulent history of Paris. The approach of bankruptcy had forced Louis XVI to convene a meeting of the Estates General, a body that had last assembled in 1614. If the king's ministers hoped that this traditional gathering could be confined to its traditional rôle they were soon undeceived. A generation reared on the speculations of the Enlightenment and inspired by the example of the American Revolution seized the chance to draft a new social contract for France and to provide an example to the whole of mankind of the translation into political practice of the humane and liberal theories that should regenerate society and inaugurate a new and happier era in the history of humanity. Throughout the country the idealists and the ambitious were eager to secure their places as the founding fathers of a new France. A country unused to politics in the modern sense, where the expression of any opinion beyond conventional thanksgiving for the virtues of the king and the wisdom of his chosen advisers was almost a form of sedition, found itself deluged by pamphlets in which hundreds of would-be Franklins and Jeffersons solved the problems of the ancient monarchy in a score of pages. At a lower level, those whose personal ambitions had been so cruelly disappointed in the previous years saw the new era as offering at least a career in political journalism, even if they could not hope for immediate success in elections where the rewards – especially in Paris – were reserved for men of established reputation and generally of substantial means.

When the deputies of the clergy, nobility and commons met in their separate Orders at Versailles in May, the atmosphere was immediately soured by a conflict between those who aspired to break down the stratification of French society and those who intended merely to graft a new political constitution on to the old social order. After weeks of deadlock the king was induced to throw the weight of the royal government behind the conservatives and was answered by the defiance of the radicals. Tension rose in nearby Paris, where the French Guards went over to the popular cause. When the king called up substantial bodies of troops to insulate Versailles from the dangerous capital, with its population of over half a million, and on 11 July dismissed his more conciliatory ministers, Paris rose against the impending coup d'état.

The capital had been divided into sixty electoral Districts, each of which had chosen a body of electors who, in a joint meeting, had elected the Parisian representatives to the Estates General. Many of these groups of electors, caught up in the political excitement, had continued to meet after their job was done and turned themselves into informal political clubs, which soon began to act as administrative bodies. When the city erupted into chaotic revolt on 12 July the electors, with surprising self-confidence and political enterprise, took control. They virtually took over the municipal government and soon raised a force of 48,000 National Guards, both to maintain order and, if need be, to defend the city against the royal troops camped just outside. It was the search for powder to arm this people's militia that led a crowd of townspeople, reinforced by some of the French Guards with artillery, to storm the Bastille, a massive symbol of the 'feudal' past and a potential royal strongpoint in the heart of working-class Paris. In the face of so much resolution, with the entire city ranged against him, Louis XVI abandoned the idea of suppressing what had now become a national revolutionary movement, dispersed his troops and appeared for a time to acquiesce in what he could no longer prevent.

Danton was not the kind of man to remain a passive spectator while a new world was being forged around him, but the record of his political activities in the first half of 1789 is a surprising blank, for which the death of his son, in April, is unlikely to be a sufficient explanation. On 18 April he defended a would-be goldsmith who was denied access to the profession on the ground that he had not served his apprenticeship. In June he successfully defended a farmer from the west who was claiming an inheritance. He was not elected to the Estates General; he was not even picked as an elector by his own District, the Cordeliers. He is said to have played some part in the café radicalism of the pleasure-grounds at the Palais Royal, owned by the Duke of Orleans, who was suspected of aspiring to dethrone his royal cousin and take his place, but Danton was less conspicuous than Desmoulins, who found his revolutionary vocation haranguing a crowd from the top of a table.

With his stentorian voice, his athletic physique and his capacity for impassioned improvisation, Danton had the qualities necessary for a successful popular orator, if he chose to use them. It looks as though he did, achieving a sudden metamorphosis that surprised his professional colleagues. Excluded from municipal, let alone national politics, he could only operate within his own District, and if he was to acquire a quick reputation, it must be by out-shouting the others. The lawyer Lavaux, writing long after the event, said that he visited the Cordelier District on 13 July.

> I saw my colleague, Danton, whom I had always known as a man of sound judgement, gentle character, modest and silent. What was my surprise at seeing him up on a table, declaiming wildly, calling the citizens to arms to repel 15,000 brigands gathered at Montmartre and an army of 30,000 poised to sack Paris and slaughter its inhabitants . . . I went up to him and asked what all the uproar was about; I spoke to him of the calm and security I had seen at Versailles. He replied that I had not understood anything, that the sovereign people had risen against despotism. 'Join us,' he said. 'The throne is over-turned and your old position is lost. Don't forget that.'[1]

Even if Danton as a pre-revolutionary lamb sounds a little uncon-vincing, his abrupt transition from public declamation to a hard-headed invitation to an old colleague to join the winning side, rings entirely true, and Danton was presumably offering Lavaux advice that he had already taken himself.

On 16 July he led a company of National Guards from the Cordeliers to the Bastille, where the new governor appointed by the Paris Commune after the capture of the fortress, refused to let him in. Outraged by this insult to the sovereign people, Danton hauled the governor before the Cordeliers and then took him to the Hôtel de Ville, where the municipal authorities immediately ordered his release. This was presumably Danton's first brush with La Fayette, who had been made Commander-in-Chief of the Parisian National Guard and was finding it impossible to enforce the kind of voluntary subordination that he had so much admired,

1. Quoted in A. Fribourg, *Discours de Danton*, Paris, 1910, p. 35.

ten years before, when serving under Washington. Trivial in itself, the incident suggests that Danton already appreciated the political capital to be gained from demonstrations of revolutionary fervour, even if they took the form of symbolic acts that produced nothing but official censure.

For what it is worth, the scanty evidence suggests that he opted for the rôle of popular leader about the time of the July crisis. With Danton, however, one can never be quite sure. At his trial, when virtually all the evidence available to the public prosecutor was drawn from the speech in which Saint-Just denounced Danton in the Assembly, Fouquier-Tinville suddenly threw in the accusation that Danton escaped to England on 17 July 1789. Saint-Just had said nothing about a voyage to England. The date is mentioned only in the unofficial bulletin of the revolutionary tribunal. There is nothing about it in Fouquier's list of evidence to be collected, and the rather disjointed notes taken by one of the jurors at the trial, Topino-Lebrun, suggest that it was merely a mistake for 1791, although, if Danton went to England then, it was in August and not in July. His historians have been unanimous in thinking that the date printed in the bulletin was simply a mistake, and they are almost certainly right, although Danton's reply to the charge: 'My brothers-in-law were going there on business and I took advantage of the opportunity', sounds a little cool if it referred to 1791 when he claimed that his life was in danger. In the French archives there is a letter from one of his half-brothers, written to him from England on 28 October 1789.[2] His step-father was a textile manufacturer who used the kind of machinery that was being produced in England and, whatever the date, Danton probably crossed the Channel with his half-brothers rather than his brothers-in-law.

All this would be unimportant and the possibility of Danton's visiting England in July 1789 too slight to be worth discussing, if it were not for one startling fact. On 26 November 1789 La Luzerne, the French Ambassador in London, reported to his Foreign Minister a conversation he had had with the Duke of Orleans, who had been shipped off to England out of the way. 'I told His Excellency that there were two English individuals in Paris, called Dantonne and Paré, whom some people suspect of

2. Archives Nationales, AF II 49.

being confidential agents of the British Government . . . I do not know if enquiries have been made to find out if these people really do exist in Paris.'[3] However one looks at it, this is a very peculiar statement indeed. There is no obvious reason why La Luzerne should have said anything of the sort to Orleans or thought it worth drawing the attention of the Foreign Minister to the fact that he had done so, unless his intention was to intimidate Orleans by letting him know that his own contacts with Danton had been exposed and that two men whom Orleans believed to be working for him were, in fact, the agents of a foreign power. The remark could have been pure invention, with the aim of blackening Danton's character, but at the time he was far too obscure – and Paré even more so – for such machiavellianism to have had much point. Whatever La Luzerne's motives and sources of information, the one disturbing fact is that someone had drawn his attention to Danton and Paré. The ambassador presumably did believe them to be Englishmen and if Danton's conduct had been such as to generate even an unjustified suspicion that he was acting as an agent of the British Government, he must have had some rather odd contacts across the Channel.

This is merely the first of a number of isolated scraps of information pointing to an ambivalence that runs through the whole of Danton's revolutionary career. Besides his relatively well-documented activities as a militant there are always hints – and sometimes much more than hints – that he was also working for the other side, or at least being paid by it. Such rumours were common currency at the time. Danton was far from being the only target for this kind of insinuation, though in his case the stories were unusually persistent. Something may have been due, as he claimed, to his contemptuous refusal to reply to calumny. His habit of conforming to revolutionary extremism in public while pursuing limited and realistic objectives in private, meant that a good deal of his activity had to remain under cover. He concealed his tracks so well that it is impossible to know what was legitimate feint and how far he allowed himself to be bribed – and whether those who paid him received any return on their investment.

Danton shared with Mirabeau not only a lack of fastidiousness about money matters but an almost instinctive grasp of the rules

3. O. Havard, *La Révolution dans les ports de guerre*, Paris, 1911, vol. II pp. 79–80.

of the new political game. When he began to play he had virtually no trumps in his hand. He was too obscure to hope for any elected office and his post as *avocat aux Conseils du Roi,* that had seemed so desirable only a couple of years before, was now a political liability. His only asset of any consequence was that he lived in a part of Paris that was becoming the centre of the new political journalism. The Cordelier District was the home of Loustalot's *Révolutions de Paris,* Fréron's *Orateur du Peuple,* Brune's *Journal de la Cour et de la Ville* and the *Mercure National,* edited by Robert and his wife. Desmoulins moved, not merely into the District, but into the same building as the Dantons, from which he edited his *Révolutions de France et de Brabant.* When Marat, the most incendiary journalist of them all, was on the run from the municipal police in the autumn of 1789, he too settled in the District in the hope of protection. This was a formidable concentration of the radical press and behind the journalists were printers like Momoro who published the violent pamphlets that launched Desmoulins on his career as a journalist.

These men formed the nucleus of the political activists of the District. Others joined them, like Fabre d'Eglantine, an ex-actor with a chequered past and a playwright of some talent, who hitched his wagon to Danton's star. Men who happened to live nearby, some of them, like Danton himself, habitués of the café Procope, swelled the numbers: the butcher, Legendre, Sergent the engraver, Ronsin, another unsuccessful dramatist, Fournier, who was known as 'the American' because of his unsuccessful speculations in the West Indies, Manuel, whose writings had earned him three months in the Bastille, the actor Collot d'Herbois; young men with a career to make, like Chaumette and Vincent. Danton's old secretary, Billaud-Varenne, was one of them and Paré followed wherever Danton led.

Not all of these men made the Cordeliers their political home from the beginning but sooner or later they gravitated there. There was a swarm of others who either remained in obscurity or dropped out of active politics. They were men of differing temperament and background but a good many came from respectable middle-class families and had been disappointed in their search for fame, or at least respectable independence in Paris. Without denying the genuine idealism of some of them, it was also true that they hoped the new order would provide them with the op-

31

portunities the old had denied them, and 1789 left them still unsatisfied. The ending of press censorship and the torrent of revolutionary journalism that followed provided opportunities for the writers, but only the exceptional men like Loustalot, Desmoulins and Marat won the kind of reputation that secured them independence. The remainder were now free to declaim at the meetings of the District and to pass revolutionary motions, but for the time being they were no more than a political nuisance to the authorities and the problem of earning a living remained as intractable as ever. It would take a new revolution if they were to attain any of their ambitions.

This group was to form Danton's political machine for the next three years. Its organisation was informal and he had no patronage at his disposal to guarantee its obedience, but this was true of most of the revolutionary parties for most of the time. The scanty records make it impossible to do more than infer the extent of Danton's control. His preference for remaining personally in the background while others executed his policies for him, makes him even more elusive. In December 1789 he wrote twice to the *Moniteur* disclaiming personal responsibility for motions that had been passed by the District. Despite all this it is clear that he quickly established his own control. When he himself moved towards the centre of Parisian politics he took a less active part in the local meetings and it would be easy to get the impression that he was neglecting the Cordeliers. The share-out of the spoils in 1792, when at last there were rewards available for the faithful, was to show, however, that the solidarity of the Cordeliers was as strong as ever. After that, it was a different matter.

By the autumn of 1789 the machine was in being. Danton had had to fight off some opposition, if the *Révolutions de Paris* was correct in saying that there were four attempts to unseat him as president, but from then onwards he was in control. An eyewitness who saw him in action on 3 October wrote afterwards:

Danton was in the chair; I had often heard of him and now I was seeing him for the first time . . . I was struck by his height and athletic build, by the irregularity of his pock-marked features, his sharp, harsh and resounding diction, his dramatic gestures and expressive features, his penetrating and confident regard, by the energy and daring of his attitude and movements . . . He presided with the decisiveness, agility and authority of a man who knows his power. He drove the assembly of the District towards his goal. It adopted a manifesto.[4]

The manifesto in question was a fierce denunciation of the king's decision to summon the Flanders Regiment to protect him at Versailles. The *Révolutions de Paris*, supporting local talent, claimed that Danton sounded the tocsin (presumably metaphorically) at the Cordeliers and the 'immortal District' stuck up a poster and formed the vanguard of the 'Parisian army' that marched to Versailles and brought the king back. The truth was rather more prosaic. The commander of the Cordelier battalion of the National Guard prevented his detachment from marching at all. Still, the Cordeliers did put up their poster and petition the municipality to order La Fayette to take his forces to Versailles. With so much of the revolutionary press concentrated within their boundaries, they were never likely to be short of publicity.

After this rather ineffective excursion into national politics, the Cordeliers concentrated their fire on the municipal government in Paris. Danton, who was presumably responsible for the tactical direction of the District, had been quick to identify the immediate enemy and the best means of harassing him. The main threat to the autonomy of the Cordeliers came not from the royal government, which had more important things to worry about, but from the mayor, Bailly, and from La Fayette, who were trying to substitute an effective municipal authority for the *ad hoc* arrangements of July. Danton realised the political capital to be made out of appeals to local autonomy and denunciations of municipal despotism. He was the inventor of what were to become the tactics of every radical group fighting for its place in the sun: the basis of all authority was the local meeting which claimed to reflect the direct democracy of the sovereign people, even if, in fact, it stood for no more than a militant minority. As far as possible, all power was to be located in such gatherings, and when concerted action on the Parisian scale was necessary, it should be taken by the spontaneous co-operation of the District (and later, of the Sections), communicating their resolutions to each other and electing *ad hoc* executive committees as necessary. All men elected

4. Quoted in Fribourg, *op. cit.*, p. 36.

to any higher body were to be delegates, not representatives, the mere agents of the Districts and subject to instant recall. Throughout the Revolution this was to be the programme of the men at the bottom. As they rose in the political hierarchy they became more impressed by the virtues of centralisation, only to find a new generation of aspiring grass-roots politicians turning their old weapons against them.

Danton realised that the confused political situation gave him a good deal of room for manoeuvre. If the municipal authorities soon developed a governmental mentality – they had, after all, to feed more than half a million people – the National Assembly (the name assumed by the Estates General in June) had the reactions of an opposition. Rightly suspecting that the king and his ministers were unwilling hostages of the Revolution, the majority of the deputies, like their humbler fellow-citizens in the Cordeliers District, proclaimed their faith in the sovereignty of the people and were obliged to tolerate disorderly popular movements for which they had little sympathy, since the only alternative was to invite the royal government to put them down. Bailly, the perplexed head of a municipality whose powers had emerged from an insurrection, had no clear basis for his authority, no precedents to appeal to and no experience of administration. Both he and La Fayette, who was similarly placed and learning the hard way that the American and French revolutions were decidedly different, could be provoked by noisy challenges into a rash assertion of authority that their tormentors could then present as a reversion to the arbitrary methods of pre-revolutionary France. If their radical opponents then appealed to the arbitration of the Assembly, the national body was unlikely to opt for any firm assertion of authority. As each particular issue petered out in confused recrimination, the Cordeliers emerged with an enhanced reputation for militancy and the defence of popular rights, while the Commune's inability to silence its challengers turned each of its formal victories into a moral defeat.

In an attempt to put the authority of the Commune on a more formal basis, Bailly invited each of the sixty Districts to nominate two men for the purpose of drafting a municipal constitution. When this draft was submitted to the Districts for their approval on 30 August, Bailly, taking their assent for granted, invited the Districts to elect five members each to the new municipal council.

Only the Cordeliers refused, on the ground that this was to anticipate the acceptance of the constitution. On 9 September they gave
way, but declared that their men were elected under protest. From
then onwards they engaged in continuous skirmishing against the
Parisian authorities. On 22 October they protested against a
scheme of La Fayette's to have delinquent National Guards judged
by courts martial. A week later the Commune censured the District
for arrogating the right to pass resolutions (when it was no more
than an informal collection of electors), for communicating its
decisions to other Districts and for imposing imperative mandates
on its representatives at the Commune. Unimpressed, the
Cordeliers voted on 12 November to impose an oath of allegiance
on their mandatories, obliging them to accept the District's right
to recall them at will. Two of their five men accepted this but the
other three refused and were replaced. When the three replace-
ments turned up at the Hôtel de Ville they were ejected and the
three who had resigned declared to be still members of the
Commune. On the following day, 17 November, the city council,
by a small majority, took the rash step of unseating Croharé, one
of the two Cordeliers who had originally accepted the imperative
mandate. This allowed the District to pose as the champion of
the freedom of election and to complain to the National Assembly
that the Commune had proclaimed its contempt for the sacred
principle of representative government. A committee of the
Assembly endorsed the position taken up by the Cordeliers but the
Assembly as a whole voted to restore the *status quo ante*. This
meant that the five men originally chosen by the Cordeliers were
all reinstated. All except Croharé promptly resigned and were
replaced by men willing to accept imperative mandates. Soon
afterwards these men resigned too and Danton and Legendre were
two of those chosen to replace them. Throughout all this complicated business the minutes of the District were regularly signed
by 'd'Anton' as its president.

On 26 December Danton led a deputation from the Cordeliers
to the Commune to denounce Bailly for awarding commissions in
the National Guard on his own authority and to allege that the
commissions referred to Bailly as *Monseigneur* (My Lord). When
Bailly replied that this was a flagrant lie, the word actually used
being the egalitarian *Monsieur*, Danton professed to have made a
mistake. Bailly probably thought this was a victory and he was

right – so far as the members of the city council and the more educated and respectable citizens were concerned. Those who were soon to be known as 'sansculottes' probably concluded that one could not be too vigilant and that Danton was on the right side, even if he made the occasional mistake.

By the end of 1789 Danton had his machine firmly in hand. On 11 December the District offered a solemn testimonial to its 'beloved president' in reply to those 'who dared to imagine that M. d'Anton was touting for votes to prolong his presidency and had purchased the unanimous support of the District'. Far from it : this unanimity was merely 'the just reward for the courage, the talent and *civisme* of which M. d'Anton has given the strongest and most shining proof, as both soldier and citizen'. The Cordeliers went on to congratulate themselves on possessing so stalwart a defender of freedom and to express their joy at being able to offer him renewed proof of their confidence in him. Even by revolutionary standards this was fulsome stuff. It was probably not written by Danton himself; his style was a good deal less florid. Fabre d'Eglantine, however, was a dramatic poet, and he signed the declaration as one of the Cordeliers' secretaries.

In the following month it was La Fayette's turn to allow the Cordeliers to make a fool of him. For some time Marat had been wanted by the police for the libels he published in his paper. On 10 October the Châtelet, the court responsible for maintaining order in Paris, which shared the unpopularity of all the pre-revolutionary institutions surviving on sufferance until the National Assembly had time to replace them, issued a warrant for Marat's arrest. He escaped by flight, first to Montmartre and then, in December, to the Cordeliers. At his invitation the District, as early as October, had declared in general terms that all writers on its territory were under its special protection. On 19 January 1790 they went a good deal further and voted that no one could be arrested within the sacred precincts of the District except with the approval of a committee of five of its members, one of whom was Danton. When this bold resolution was voted the president was not Danton. It was Paré.

On 22 January La Fayette fell into the trap and sent a small army of 3,000 men with two cannon to arrest Marat. The Cordeliers refused to give him up and there was an awkward confrontation in the street. Danton perhaps thought it wiser not to test the legality of the resolution of 19 January. When the two policemen who had been ordered to make the arrest produced their warrant, Danton's delicate sense of legal propriety was shocked to discover that it was the old warrant of 10 October, which he professed to believe had been invalidated by subsequent legislation. He talked the policemen into agreeing to refer the matter to the Assembly, and while the deputies were being consulted, La Fayette's 3,000 National Guards stood around looking foolish. With unusual promptitude and resolution the Assembly came down on the side of the Parisian authorities. Danton, his conscience and his scruples assuaged, then invited the forces of law and order to proceed with the arrest of Marat who, by this time, was well on his way to England.

The Châtelet had no more sense than to try again. On 17 March they issued a warrant against Danton himself, for inciting the District to protect Marat in defiance of the law. Accounts vary as to what Danton had actually said, but he was not a lawyer for nothing. He had probably put it in the conditional tense and, in any case, had he done more than give an assembly of the sovereign people the benefit of his opinion? The Cordeliers were naturally shocked at such disregard for constitutional principle and 300 of them signed a petition on Danton's behalf. Even the Commune, which probably did not share their views about their *chéri président*, felt that the Châtelet had gone too far, and supported the protest. As usual, the business was referred to the Assembly, which was at least becoming familiar with Danton's name. Once again a committee declared in his favour but the Assembly declined to intervene and the whole business lapsed.

Out-manoeuvred by the Cordeliers on every occasion, the Parisian authorities deployed their final weapon. In May 1790 they persuaded the Assembly to abolish the Districts and divide Paris into forty-eight Sections. The Districts had a shadowy claim to have been invested with a share of popular sovereignty, on account of their revolutionary origins in the summer of 1789. The Sections were the creation of the Assembly; their rôle was defined by law and their powers strictly circumscribed. Only 'active citizens' (those who paid a minimum of three days' wages in direct taxation) were entitled to attend; they were to meet only for the purpose of elections or when requested by at least fifty of their members. The District of the Cordeliers now took in the working-class population by the bank of the Seine and became the Théâtre français Section. They could probably have absorbed the new-comers and the exclusion of 'passive citizens', since the really poor played little part in revolutionary politics, but they were destroyed by the limitations imposed on their activities. They answered the blow as best they could, reconstituting themselves as the Cordelier Club, with a very low subscription, designed to attract a different clientèle from that of the elegant and respectable Jacobins. The new club was directed by the men who had dominated the District and it was to have its moments of importance if not of glory. Nevertheless, the abolition of the Districts had been a shrewd move. The club had no constitutional standing and could not exploit the nebulous claim to be a part of the municipal constitution that had served the District so well. It was essentially an organ of propaganda, but since it was rarely visited by important politicians it could not hope to influence legislation, like the Jacobins. It was only important in times of crisis and its only effective weapon was the threat of insurrection.

Danton, understandably, decided that it was not a particularly useful instrument for his virtuoso performances on the brink of legality, and never took a very active part in its activities. By now he was a member of the Jacobins, where he made his first recorded speech in May 1790, and he had set his sights on penetrating the municipal government that he had previously harassed so effectively. None the less, the club met practically on his doorstep. Its leaders were all members of his political machine. In moments of crisis they turned to him for guidance. He did not need to be present himself to direct its operations and for the first two years of its existence it was securely under his control.

III The Pursuit of Office

When the political machine that Danton had created lost most of its immediate purpose, with the abolition of the Districts in the summer of 1790, he changed his tactics and began to campaign for election to the Paris Commune itself. He then made the unpleasant discovery that the qualities which had made him the idol of the militants in the Théâtre français Section had an opposite effect on a wider electorate. In August 1790 the Parisians were called upon to choose a mayor, a *procureur* and two deputy *procureurs*. The election was a triumph for Bailly who was returned with 12,550 votes. Danton got forty-nine. His own Section deserted him, for Bailly collected 478 of the 580 votes polled in the Théâtre français. Even if Danton was not a declared candidate, as some of his biographers have suggested, this was scarcely encouraging. The election of the *procureur* and his deputies was almost as disappointing. Danton's successful opponents polled 3,452, 2,961 and 2,332 votes, while he received 129, 193 and 197 (less than half the voting strength of Théâtre français alone). Worse was to follow. In September his section chose him as one of its three representatives on the new municipal council. All those elected had to be endorsed by the Sections as a whole. So far as the others were concerned, this was a mere formality. Danton was the only one of 144 councillors to be rejected, and by no less than forty-three of the forty-eight Sections. This certainly indicated that he had acquired a Parisian reputation, but not one that looked like doing him much good.

The election results showed that there was something special about Danton. Perhaps his following, even in his own Section, was confined to a militant minority and was liable to be overturned on any occasion when those who had boycotted the meetings of the old District, and now kept away from the club, took the trouble to vote. Perhaps those who applauded him as an agitator preferred to be administered by someone more reassuring. This still leaves something to be explained. There were more than 197 radicals amongst the Parisian voters and the quite specific rejection of Danton as an individual by all but five of the Sections must indicate more than political conservatism, even if he was a particular target for La Fayette's pamphleteers. The most likely explanation of his unpopularity is the strength of the rumours that his private activities were very different from his public declamations. He was said to be working for the Duke of Orleans, who was credited with being the head of a mysterious party about which much has been hinted and virtually nothing proved; for Mirabeau, whom almost everyone admired and no one trusted; even for the court itself.[1] The former Grub Street hacks had not lost their old habits when they became the journalists of the Revolution and the air was thick with insinuations against almost everybody who was worth buying; even the 'incorruptible' Robespierre was accused of being in the pay of the court in 1792. If stories of this kind were indeed the main reason for Danton's exclusion, they must have been unusually persistent.

The Paris municipality was, in theory at least, subordinated to the Department, which took in some of the surrounding countryside as well as the city itself. The reorganisation of local government involved the election of a new Departmental council. This time Danton was successful. In October 1790 he recovered his grip on his own Section, which made him the second of its twenty-six electors and in the following January – admittedly after eight recounts – he secured a place on the council. This surprising reversal of the ostracism he had had to endure in the autumn has been attributed to his having joined Mirabeau's undercover organisation and benefited from Mirabeau's protection. The fact itself is likely enough but no one has ever explained how it could have had such an effect on voters who were not in the habit of accepting political guidance. Danton's election to the council of the Department was poor consolation for his failure to win actual office in the Commune. He was never put on any of the Department's committees, he was a poor attender and his election brought him neither profit nor influence.

At least the old guard remained faithful. When the Districts had been replaced by the Sections, the National Guard had not been brought into line and was still organised in sixty battalions, each corresponding to one of the original Districts. Towards the end of 1790 the Cordelier battalion chose Danton to be its com-

1. For a discussion of these charges, see Chapter 4.

manding officer. There was some controversy and Aulard believed the opposition was such that Danton resigned, but in April 1791 he was reported by an eye-witness as being still at the head of the battalion. In Paris as a whole, feeling against him remained hostile. When he stood for election as judge in one of the new courts, in November, he received five votes. It was perhaps hardly the kind of office most suited to his particular talents. This reverse was all the more serious since his old office as *avocat aux Conseils du Roi* had been suppressed in the general reorganisation of the legal system. His last known case was in March and he received his financial compensation in July. After that, apart from collecting outstanding fees, he had no known source of income. At the end of 1790 the resignation of the second deputy *procureur* gave him another chance to try his luck. This time he did rather better, getting 386 votes against the winner's 1,558. With such a small fraction of the electorate troubling to vote, there was always the possibility of a sudden reversal of the majority, but everything suggested that he still had a very long way to go. His persistent and ignominious failure to secure a post on the Commune certainly makes his election to the Department rather surprising.

Throughout 1790 and 1791 he continued to play the radical card, though it never won him any tricks. In October 1790 there was a movement in the Assembly against the king's ministers. Although a vote of no confidence was defeated, the resolution that was passed, expressing confidence in the Foreign Minister alone, was a condemnation of the others. This debate set off agitation in the Paris Sections. Mauconseil, one of the five that had been prepared to approve Danton, launched a campaign against the ministers, that won the support of a majority of the Sections. A committee was set up to draft a petition to the Assembly. Sergent, Danton's friend and a member of the Cordelier club, was its president and Danton its secretary. Since the petition had the support of a majority of the Sections, the reluctant Bailly was obliged to lead the deputation that took it to the Assembly, but it was Danton who delivered – and perhaps wrote – the address, on 11 November.

He began by claiming that the Assembly had the right to dismiss ministers (who were, in theory, advisers chosen by the king and responsible to him). This was immediately challenged by the two royalist leaders, the abbé Maury and Cazalès, whose attack

41

won Danton the sympathy of the majority. He went on to claim for Paris the special position that it was to demand throughout the Revolution. 'This Commune, composed of citizens who belong, in a manner of speaking, to the eighty-three Departments . . .' This set off another uproar. Once again, as in the claims he had advanced in the previous year, for the autonomy of the Districts, Danton had invented what was to become the orthodox doctrine of the militants – while they were in opposition. He went on, not merely to denounce the majority of the ministers, but to demand the creation of a High Court before which three of them should be sent for trial. The Assembly agreed to receive the petition but did nothing about it. Nevertheless, the three ministers all resigned within a couple of months. Danton could regard it as a victory of sorts, all the more comforting since it was his only one.

His few known speeches at the Jacobins consisted of attacks on the more moderate members of the club. On 30 March 1791 he even criticised a fellow-Cordelier, Collot d'Herbois, for praising a Jacobin who had agreed to accept a diplomatic post. His assertion that no one who accepted any kind of office could be a good Jacobin was too radical even for Robespierre, who nevertheless supplied him with a kind of testimonial: 'I know M. Danton to be a good citizen, but I cannot agree with him in this particular case.' In May he attacked three of the more conservative members of the club. His eulogy of Mirabeau, who died on 2 April, need not signify anything in particular; despite the rumours already circulating that he had been bought by the court, Mirabeau's death reminded all the revolutionaries of his defiance of the royal government, when that still required some courage, in 1789, and there was a general chorus of praise in which even Robespierre joined.

April 1791 brought an incident, minor in itself, which illuminates Danton's use of his machine for publicity purposes and perhaps helps to explain why so many people found his methods so distasteful. The Assembly had blundered into a conflict with the Church, and its new Civil Constitution of the Clergy was rejected by almost all the bishops and about half the parish priests. Although Louis XVI put his signature to it, he had qualms of conscience about it and began making serious preparations to escape from Paris. Presumably as a public gesture, he decided to retire to Saint-Cloud for his Easter communion, although he could have had the services of a priest who rejected the Civil Constitution, without leaving Paris. Since there were rumours that the king's real intention was to escape from France altogether, when the royal party prepared to leave their palace on 17 April an angry and suspicious crowd unharnessed the horses. The National Guard detachments on duty, which included the battalion from the Cordeliers, were hesitant and reluctant to drive back the crowds by force. Bailly and La Fayette turned for advice to the Department, which in turn decided to consult the Sections. All this took time and after a humiliating wait in their coaches the royal family eventually admitted defeat and returned to the Tuileries.

Danton was probably present at the head of the Cordeliers battalion, though there is no evidence that he did anything in particular. In the evening he made a fairly non-committal report of the business to the Jacobins. One newspaper even quoted him as having disapproved of the crowd's action, though this seems unlikely. Ten days later, he presented a very different story to his Section. He claimed then that, when Bailly and La Fayette went to the Department they demanded permission to proclaim martial law and order the National Guards to fire on the crowd if necessary. According to Danton, his vigorous intervention reduced them to silence. Suitably impressed and determined to publicise its old hero's activities, Théâtre français posted up this version throughout Paris. Desmoulins, who, like other revolutionary journalists, considered that the guidance he offered his readers extended to facts as well as opinion, attributed to Danton and Kersaint a stern letter to the king that had actually been written by Talleyrand and Pastoret.[2]

At the meeting of the Department on 7 May Danton was invited to comment on the Théâtre français poster. He began by a tactical retreat, disclaiming any responsibility for the particular words attributed to him, but endorsing the general sense of the poster. At the invitation of his colleagues he produced a written statement that was a masterpiece of evasion: 'At a meeting with several members of the Department, in one of the rooms of the National Assembly, in the course of discussions with the mayor and the commandant-general they seemed to me, in their proposals,

2. For the best account see A. Schmidt, *Tableau de la Révolution Française*, Leipzig, 1867, Vol. I, pp. 17 *et seq.*

to hold consistently to the opinion that the king's departure should be protected by the armed forces.' Even this was a piece of impudence. The Department had already established that there had been two meetings on 17 April. Danton had not been present at the first of these, which took place while the crowd was milling round the royal coach. He *had* attended the second meeting, but by the time that took place the royal family was back in the Tuileries, the crowd had dispersed and no one had mentioned a proclamation of martial law, which would no longer have served any purpose. The Department, presumably under the impression that Danton's exposure was sufficient punishment in itself, decided to take no action against the poster of Théâtre français, which allowed Danton's version of events to remain in circulation. He was still repeating it at the time of his trial and some of his historians have taken him at his own word.

Two months later, on the night of 20–21 June, the royal family really did escape, although they were recaptured after a couple of days. The news that they had left Paris plunged the revolutionaries into confusion. The leaders of the majority in the Assembly, Barnave, Duport and the Lameth brothers, were moderate men aspiring to create a constitutional monarchy roughly similar to that of England. This was also the ambition of Bailly and La Fayette. Such men had appeared radical in 1789 when they had accepted popular insurrection in order to overthrow absolutism. Two years later they judged that this battle had been won and they were becoming increasingly concerned by the continuing instability in the countryside and growing social unrest in Paris, where the spring had brought an outbreak of strikes. After Mirabeau's death in April they tried to negotiate a compromise with the king, hoping that this would allow them to bring the Revolution to an end. All their plans were endangered by the flight of the royal family which threatened an open breach between the king and the Assembly, civil war, and perhaps foreign invasion, if the Habsburg Emperor, Leopold II, responded to the urgent pleas of his sister, Marie Antoinette, to come to her rescue. The constitutional monarchists immediately decided to pretend that the irreparable had not happened. They persuaded the Assembly to declare, however implausibly, that the king had been 'abducted'. This fiction would have been quickly exposed if he had not been recaptured. His arrest put him at the Assembly's mercy and he was only too ready to accept the lifeline that was thrown to him. He pretended that he had formed the mistaken impression that the Revolution had not been accepted by the country as a whole. His travels had convinced him that the contrary was the case and he was prepared to accept the national verdict. The Assembly eventually 'suspended' him until it should have finished drafting the constitution, on the understanding that he would be restored to the throne if he accepted it.

The Jacobin club, where the moderates had a majority in numbers, if not in talent, was prepared to accept this compromise and save the king's face. A minority, led by Robespierre, objected to any attempt to buy the king's agreement by revising the constitution in his favour and suspected the Lameths and their supporters of being mainly concerned with gaining power for themselves. It was easy for Robespierre to expose the shabby fictions of his opponents, but he had no alternative policy to offer since he preferred a weak monarchy to a republic dominated by his political opponents. As the crisis developed he came to believe that the moderates were looking for a pretext for a confrontation that would allow them to suppress the Parisian radicals by force. While bitterly attacking their leaders, he was concerned to prevent the Jacobins from falling into what he saw as a trap, and to ensure that their policy remained strictly within the limits of the law.

There may have been some who hoped to use the crisis to obtain a change of dynasty, putting Orleans on the throne. Besides the duke's own coterie, who perhaps thought in terms of furthering their own careers, it was quite reasonable for disinterested revolutionaries to take the view that he would make a more convincing constitutional monarch than the discredited Louis, although anyone rash enough to suggest this in public was liable to find himself denounced as a paid agent of Orleans.

There remained a third possibility: to accept the king's flight as an act of abdication and proclaim a republic. This had the kind of simple logic that appealed to unsophisticated men of a radical temper. As the cartoons of the period show, with their penchant for portraying the royal family transformed into a litter of pigs, the king and queen had been permanently discredited by their flight and were now regarded with both hatred and contempt. There seemed little practical difference between a republic and a constitutional monarchy based on a sovereign Assembly and a suspended king. In actual fact things were not so simple. Apart from the risk of war and its unpredictable consequences for the Revolution, to abolish the monarchy would have destroyed the constitution that had been two years in the making. Everything would have been thrown into confusion. This was more likely to appeal to the militants of Théâtre français than to the moderate men in control of the Assembly.

From whatever motives, the Cordelier club began to campaign, if not specifically for a republic, at least against any attempt to whitewash the king. During the previous few months the club had helped to bring into being a number of fraternal societies that had spread the revolutionary gospel amongst working people.[3] In May a central committee of these societies had been established, meeting in the same building as the Cordeliers, with Robert as its first president. This committee had supported a wave of strikes. By the time of the king's flight the Cordeliers had therefore considerably extended their influence in Paris, though they could not rely on being able to control the new forces they had brought into being.

For Danton, this looked like the parting of the ways. His only secure base was in the Cordelier club but his hopes of election in Paris and of an eventual career on the national stage could only be attained with Jacobin support. To toe the Jacobin line now promised safety but no rewards. Too open an endorsement of Jacobin caution might endanger his control of the machine he had created, just when it was extending its influence over much of the left bank of the Seine. To lead a militant republican movement would lose him the Jacobins and meant risking everything, from ostracism to possible execution, on the outcome of an unpredictable gamble. His response to this dilemma was very much in character. He kept himself informed about everything and at the centre of events in both camps; when he spoke in public it was to make violent denunciations that never quite committed him to anything in particular; when there was action to be taken he left it to his friends.

His immediate reaction to the king's flight was a fierce attack

3. See A. Mathiez, *Le club des Cordeliers pendant la crise de Varennes et le massacre du Champ de Mars*, Paris, 1910, *passim*.

in the Jacobins on 21 June, not against the king, but against La Fayette who was responsible for the patrols around the Tuileries that had failed to catch the fugitives. Danton insinuated that La Fayette's attitudes and policies were suspiciously like those of Louis. After a melodramatic opening, in which he demanded death for unspecified traitors and asserted that the flight was part of a vast plot that owed its success to the connivance of the leading public authorities, the rest of his speech was a continuous diminuendo. La Fayette was either a traitor or a fool, but Danton charitably assumed him to be no more than the latter and merely invited him to resign. He then demanded sweeping measures to save the Revolution, but the only one he actually proposed was to expel from the Assembly those members who had proclaimed their opposition to the constitution. This would, in practice, have strengthened the position of the moderate constitutional monarchists. When Alexandre de Lameth objected that he had always considered La Fayette to be a faithful supporter of the constitution, Danton contented himself with agreeing that this was how Lameth had always spoken to him about La Fayette. This did not get anyone very far. Desmoulins, in the melodramatic version of the scene that he presented to his readers, told them that he had wanted to jump up and tell the Jacobins that Lameth, who was now defending La Fayette, had previously urged Desmoulins to attack him. Danton, who was sitting next to him, stopped him.

In the meantime the Cordeliers, at Robert's invitation, decided to petition the Assembly to take no action about the king's flight – unless it decided to proclaim a republic – until the country as a whole had been consulted. The Jacobins took the news of this very badly, some of their members proposing to sever all relations with the Cordeliers until they had withdrawn their petition. Danton persuaded the Jacobins to take no action. He must have been wondering how long he could go on playing for both sides at once. A member of the Jacobins then proposed that La Fayette should be invited to reply to the rhetorical questions Danton had put to him on the previous night and Danton was asked to set them down in writing. He appeared to agree but then declined, with the curious argument that, since he had made all the advances towards La Fayette by inviting him to explain his conduct, the next move was up to La Fayette. This amounted to rather less than the demolition of La Fayette with which some of Danton's admirers have credited him.

On 23 June, when the king's recapture was known, the Jacobins discussed what the Assembly should do when he was brought back to Paris. Replying to a member who said that Louis was still king, Danton once again took refuge in ambiguity. As in the case of La Fayette, he maintained that Louis was either criminal or mad; the revolutionaries should adopt the more indulgent assumption and instead of dethroning him and replacing him by a regent ruling in the name of his infant son, should opt for a *conseil à l'interdiction*, to be chosen by the Departments. This does not seem to have attracted much interest or support; most of the members had probably very little idea of what would be involved in practice. It was an ingenious compromise that would have humiliated Louis while still keeping open the possibility of restoring him to the throne when he had 'recovered'. It was probably too ingenious, in the sense that it frustrated the hopes of compromisers, Orleanists and republicans. When the Jacobins returned to the subject, on 3 July, Danton again opposed a regency, this time in favour of a 'sequestration of the vacant throne', whatever that may have been intended to imply. He was presumably laying down a smokescreen at the Jacobins, maintaining a radical pose while not committing himself to anything in particular. This was all very well as far as it went, but he was in danger of losing touch with his Cordelier flank.

In Paris, a popular republican movement, encouraged by the Cordeliers and the fraternal societies, was rapidly gaining ground while the Assembly debated what to do with the king. Republicanism took the only channel open to it: the organisation of repeated petitions to the Assembly, whose signature provided the occasion for a number of mass meetings. When a petition that the Assembly should consult the electorate before taking any decision was handed in on 24 June, four of the seven men who presented it came from the Cordeliers. On 9 July the club submitted a petition of its own, which Charles Lameth, who was in the chair, refused to transmit to the Assembly. As the deputies gradually moved towards a decision, tension mounted and the Cordeliers became more agitated. On 12 July they adopted a proposal by Chaumette to invite the electors (originally convened before the king's escape, to choose the deputies to the next Assembly) to disregard their prorogation by the present Assembly and to elect a provisional government. As the language of the Cordeliers became more insurrectionary, Danton raised the temperature at the Jacobins with a denunciation of kings in general and of those like Duport who wanted to restore Louis to his throne. He dismissed the argument that dethroning Louis would risk a catastrophic foreign war and, if one can believe the *Journal de la Révolution,* concluded with the threat: 'Let the Assembly tremble . . . The Nation, born anew in freedom, is a Hercules who will crush the serpents seeking to devour it!' To do him justice, Danton was far from being the only revolutionary to favour this kind of Delphic utterance which, after the event, if things had gone the right way, one could always claim to have been the clarion call that launched an insurrection.

On 15 July the Cordeliers and the fraternal societies held a meeting on the Champ de Mars to collect signatures to another petition. Delegates were sent to the Assembly where Robespierre and Pétion told them that since the deputies had now voted to keep the king on the throne, a petition would be out of order. Unconvinced, the delegates and their supporters moved off to the society of *Friends of Truth,* where a mass meeting voted not to recognise any decree absolving Louis XVI, and from there to the Jacobins. Danton, who was at the Jacobins, must have found this particularly awkward, as his two worlds converged on each other. He told the Jacobins that since a petition was merely the expression of an opinion, it could not be regarded as unconstitutional to go on petitioning after the Assembly had made its will known. With the kind of legalistic ingenuity that had proved its usefulness in 1790 he went on to argue that, in any case, the decree of the Assembly was expressed in such obscure and involuted language that the bewildered citizenry had every right to ask for its elucidation. Perhaps sensing that this appeasement of Jacobin caution was not going down very well with their visitors from the Cordeliers and the fraternal societies, he ended on a note of defiance. 'Those who are afraid of raising their heads like free men don't need to sign. Don't we need a purge? This is it.' This was too much for the Jacobins. The great majority of the members took him at his word and walked out, to found a new club of their own. The rump elected a committee of five, including Danton and Sergent, to decide whether a petition was still legal. Not surprisingly they concluded that it was.

At the Champ de Mars on 16 July Danton seems to have been one of those who read the Jacobin petition to the crowd. Someone had tacked on to the end of it a proposal to replace Louis 'by constitutional means', which presumably implied a regency for his son, with Orleans as regent. The Cordeliers and the Friends of Truth insisted on having this deleted. Since the petition came from the Jacobins, it now had to go back to the club for the amended version to be approved. In the meantime a deputation that included the three Cordeliers, Billaud-Varenne, Desmoulins and Fréron, went to inform the municipal authorities that there was to be another meeting at the Champ de Mars on the following day. At this point Jacobins and Cordeliers finally broke apart. The Cordeliers admittedly turned down a motion to make the meeting of the 17th a 'demonstration in arms' (less euphemistically, an insurrection), but they insisted on a petition. The Jacobins, after first insisting on restoring the clause about 'constitutional means', eventually decided to drop the whole idea of a petition as illegal. It looked as though Danton was going to have to choose.

During the forenoon of 17 July Sergent, who was president of Théâtre français, called at Danton's home and found him with Desmoulins, Fréron, Brune, Fabre d'Eglantine, Momoro and Santerre, a wealthy brewer from the radical faubourg Saint-Antoine. This meeting of the general staff of the Cordeliers was interrupted by Legendre, bringing a message that had come indirectly from Alexandre de Lameth, advising them to get out of Paris for the day. Danton, Desmoulins and Fréron promptly left for a house in the country that belonged to Danton's father-in-law.

In the meantime the crowd that assembled on the Champ de Mars was told that the Jacobins had withdrawn their petition. Those of the Cordeliers who had turned up presented yet another petition, written by Robert, demanding the king's trial and the election of a new constituent assembly. Amongst the 6,000 who signed were Sergent, Momoro, Santerre, Hébert and Chaumette. While this was going on, the municipality, taking advantage of the lynching of two Peeping Toms at the Champ de Mars earlier in the day, had proclaimed martial law. Bailly and La Fayette led a force of National Guards to the scene of the petitioning. A shot was heard and the National Guards opened fire on the crowd. No one knows how many were killed; the militants put the figure in thousands but it was probably rather less than fifty.

The 'massacre' was the signal for a general proscription of the radicals. Martial law remained in force for weeks. Warrants were issued for the arrest of Desmoulins, Santerre, Brune, Momoro and other Cordeliers but not, at first, for Danton. His rôle in the business had been something less than heroic. He had kept away from the meeting at the Champ de Mars that he knew to be dangerous, without trying to prevent it. If the authorities had left him alone, this might have discredited him in the eyes of the Cordeliers. Most obligingly, on 4 August they made a – painless – martyr of him. Significantly enough, despite the witch-hunt taking place at the time, he was not accused of anything relating to the Champ de Mars affair. On 21 June, the day the king's flight was discovered, while walking to a meeting of the Department, allegedly with an armed guard, Danton was said to have called to an angry crowd that was demanding La Fayette's head, 'You are right. Your leaders are all traitors who are deceiving you.' This was a flimsy enough charge and no one had bothered to do anything about it for six weeks. It may be that the main intention of the authorities, in the case of Danton and his lieutenants, was merely to keep them out of the way during the elections to the next Assembly. They were quite successful in that respect but they presented Danton with a useful certificate of persecution.

He made his way to Arcis, where he was sheltered by Courtois, who was to be elected to the new Assembly, and thence to Troyes. The local authorities seem to have treated him as something of a hero but there were limits to the protection they could offer against an arrest warrant. If he really did go to England, as was alleged at his trial, it was probably at this time, but nothing is known of how long he stayed or what he did there.

During his absence the faithful Théâtre français chose him as one of its electors. This provided him with the kind of semi-public character that he knew so well how to exploit. He returned to Paris and presented himself at the meeting of all the electors of Paris. Damien, one of the policemen the Cordeliers had humiliated when they tried to arrest Marat in 1790, tried to serve the warrant. Outraged by this lack of respect for popular sovereignty, the electors ordered the arrest of the unfortunate Damien, who appealed to the Assembly. So did Danton. This set off a formal joust in which the deputies paraded their constitutional principles in favour of one side or the other. Robespierre defended the electors and said nothing about Damien. The Assembly voted the other way, releasing Damien and saying nothing about Danton. Since they voted a general amnesty to celebrate the king's acceptance of the constitution, Danton's prosecution lapsed automatically and he was back in play. He did not, however, manage to get himself elected to the Legislative Assembly.

On the whole he had emerged from a difficult situation remarkably well. He was still the leader of the Cordeliers and he had not forfeited the confidence of those who remained in the Jacobins. He could claim, as he did at his trial, that his arrest had been ordered 'on account of the Champ de Mars'. It was not quite true but it was accurate enough to pass muster. Robespierre, in 1794, was to reproach him with supporting the 'constitutional means' amendment and to allege that he only escaped arrest because of a private understanding with the authorities. He did not say anything of the voyage to England, which would have supplied useful 'evidence' of Danton's participation in a foreign plot. This is another reason for wondering whether it ever happened, at least in 1791. In 1794 Robespierre knew that Danton's acquittal would mean the overthrow of the government and he could not afford to be unduly scrupulous about his choice of weapons. He knew all the facts in 1791 and they did not prevent him from working with Danton for the next two and a half years and presenting him with the occasional testimonial.

After the bloody crisis of the summer, life returned to normal. For Danton, this meant the pursuit of office. However incensed they may have been by the misplaced zeal of Damien, the Paris electors did not choose his victim to represent them in the new Assembly. Danton does not seem to have stood when Bailly resigned as mayor and was replaced by Pétion, but he tried his luck in the election of a new *procureur* in November 1791. The Cordeliers invited the Jacobins to support their candidate but were put in their place for improper canvassing and Danton came an inglorious third. Manuel, a former Cordelier, was elected. In December there was a new election, to replace the second of Manuel's deputies, and Danton tried again. Villain d'Aubigny canvassed the Jacobins on his behalf and received a lesson from the scrupulous Robespierre, who was courteous enough to say that he had intended to object before Danton's name was mentioned. Since, within a matter of weeks, Robespierre was to remind the Jacobins of the virtues of Buzot and Antoine, candidates for election to the criminal court, there may have been more to his reluctance to endorse Danton than constitutional propriety. A little later Danton must have enjoyed pointing out to the club that its proposal to despatch copies of one of Robespierre's speeches to the army would be a breach of the law.

Even without the support of the Jacobins, Danton managed to beat Collot d'Herbois by 1,162 votes to 654. In a city with an electorate of something like 80,000, this could scarcely be described as a landslide and the office itself was not particularly important since Manuel left his deputies little scope, but Danton had at last managed to get elected to *something* and the post would bring him in a useful 6,000 livres a year. When, in the early days of 1792, his friends Panis and Sergent also entered the Commune and were put on the police committee, the Cordeliers were quite well entrenched within the Paris Commune.

Danton celebrated his election with a curious inaugural address. He began by claiming that an enlightened public had sought him out, as a man of purity, in the rural retreat to which he had retired. The absence of any signs of his activity in Paris between mid-September and mid-December confirms this suggestion that he may have retired to the Aube, where he had bought an estate of some size. It was proof of his innocence – or impudence – that he himself drew attention to this purchase 'which my detractors have magnified into enormous estates, paid for by goodness knows what agents of England and Russia'. In a general policy statement he said that his aim was to reassure those who 'wanted liberty but were afraid of tempests' by a profession of his true principles.

> Nature provided me with the athletic build and the rough features of liberty. Free from the misfortune of being born into one of those races which our former institutions treated as privileged . . . as I made my own way I retained all my native vigour without ceasing for a second, in my private life or my profession, to show that I knew how to combine the sang-froid of reason with warmth of spirit and strength of character.

Having awarded himself this testimonial as a self-made man, he confessed that at the beginning of the Revolution he had 'consented to appear an extremist since he would never be a weakling'.

He explained to the timid friends of liberty whom he wanted to reassure, that he had not shared their generous credulity when facing politicians whom he suspected of hiding political ambition beneath the appearance of principle. They in turn had persecuted him in 1789, slandered him since and persecuted him again in 1791 – he did not pretend on this occasion that it was for anything directly connected with the events on the Champ de Mars. All this he had had to endure 'because I always act in accordance with the eternal laws of justice and I am incapable of maintaining a relationship that has become impure'. Henceforth, his watchword was to be: 'The constitution, nothing but the constitution'. He warned the king against toying with the idea of counter-revolution, which was the only threat to the peace of France, and he ended by threatening the tyrants of the world with extermination if they did not abandon their intrigues against the Revolution. On the whole, the timid friends of liberty must have found this mildly reassuring. It sounded as though Danton was prepared to make the best of an imperfect job and to accept the constitution as it stood. He had got some of what he wanted, even if he had no means of satisfying the appetites of his fellow-Cordeliers. What must have sounded less convincing was his emphasis on his purity. There were two opinions about that.

IV The Double Agent

According to Danton, he was one of the leading radicals with whom La Fayette discussed the political situation in the summer of 1790, presumably in the hope of enlisting their support. The leader of the Parisian National Guard pointed out to Danton that his noisy histrionics in the Cordelier District had not done him any good; he had succeeded in excluding himself from municipal office by 'a kind of ostracism on the part of the Sections', while his enemy, Bailly, was triumphantly re-elected as mayor. No one has ever accused Danton of naïveté and he was the last man to need reminding that he did not seem to be getting anywhere. His subsequent career showed that he liked to keep all his options open and avoided making political enemies whenever he could. If he rejected La Fayette's overtures he must have had his reasons. The most likely explanation was some sort of an understanding with La Fayette's bitter rival, Mirabeau – and behind Mirabeau stood the court.

This raises the question of Danton's venality, the source of so much savage controversy. The early historians of the Revolution took his corruption for granted, the positivists thought they had refuted it and Mathiez believed he had proved it beyond any doubt. The argument, however distorted by the determination of most of the participants to vindicate the conclusions with which they started out, has at least had the merit of encouraging both sides to uncover an impressive amount of evidence.[1] This has to be approached with caution. If one rejects the positivist view of Danton as a latter-day Joan of Arc one has to resist the temptation to go to the opposite extreme, with Mathiez, and assume that any sort of discreditable rumour gains credibility by the mere fact that Danton is its target. Villain d'Aubigny recorded a typical example of such malicious gossip. He was present when Bourdon de l'Oise claimed to have documentary proof that Danton had bought sequestrated church property to the value of almost a

1. For the best summary, see G. Lefebvre, 'Sur Danton', in *Annales historiques de la Révolution française*, 1932, reprinted in *Etudes sur la Révolution française*, Paris, 1954.

million livres. When Danton himself arrived and challenged him, Bourdon was forced to admit that his 'documentary proof' amounted to no more than hearsay.[2] Even allowing for the revolutionary mania for wholesale denunciation, however, the persistence of the rumours about Danton must raise the suspicion that so much smoke must indicate some sort of fire.

Two lines of investigation are possible: to see if Danton's finances suggest that he came into possession of inexplicable sources of money, and to seek positive evidence that he was being secretly paid by those whom he pretended to attack in public. Each of these presents its own difficulties. His political enemies cannot be assumed to have been telling the truth merely because they incriminated Danton and there is always the possibility that some of his legitimate sources of income may have gone unrecorded. None the less, a combination of the two lines of enquiry leads to conclusions that are rather more than conjecture.

When Danton bought the office that launched him on his career he had to find a total of 78,000 livres plus legal expenses, 66,000 almost at once and the remaining 12,000, plus interest, over a period of four years.[3] He paid in cash the whole of the 66,000, together with 2,400 of the 12,000 outstanding (which was supposed to represent debts owed to Huet de Paisy, who sold him the office). He found the money by raising a loan of 10,000 livres on the security of the office, to be repaid in 1792, and borrowing 36,000 from Mlle Duhauttoir, repayable in stages by 1795. The remainder came from his wife's dowry. On the assumption that Huet's debts were recovered in full, the 2,400 that Danton had already paid him would be available towards the reimbursement of his own debts and would leave him with another 43,600 to find.

If Danton had paid a reasonable price for his office (which is to disregard the fact that Huet himself had paid less than half as much for it only thirteen years earlier), it could be expected to yield an annual income of about 5 per cent of its purchase price, in other words, about 4,000 livres a year. Danton paid 1,040 livres

2. *Villain d'Aubigny, membre du comité révolutionnaire de la Section des Tuileries et adjoint au Ministre de la Guerre à Philippeaux.* Paris, an II, p. 19n[1].
3. See G. Pioro, 'Sur la fortune de Danton', *Annales historiques de la Révolution française*, 1955.

for the annual rent of his flat, which he had to furnish. When his wife died in the spring of 1793 the possessions of the couple were valued at just over 9,000 livres, with Danton's library worth another 2,800. Assuming, on the basis of the fact that his library was mentioned in his marriage contract, that he bought no more books between 1787 and 1793, and allowing for the depreciation of the currency, which would inflate the 1793 estimate, he must have been acquiring furniture and household effects at an annual rate of at least 1,000 livres a year. The running expenses of his home and his legal office can scarcely have cost him less than another 2,000 and they probably amounted to considerably more. Even if he paid no interest on his mortgage, which is unlikely, his annual expenditure must have been at least 4,000 livres and may well have been much higher.

It is, of course, possible that Danton's exceptional talent and energy may have revived a legal practice that Huet had neglected, but in view of the demands of his political activities, from the autumn of 1789 onwards, this is hardly likely. Fribourg, who edited his speeches, was able to find traces of only twenty-two cases in which he was involved, between the purchase of his office and its suppression in 1791. With the best will in the world, it is difficult to see how he could have been more than barely solvent. Nevertheless, in December 1789 he paid off the 9,600 livres outstanding from his debt of 12,000, together with 1,500 in interest, although he had until 1791 in which to pay. There is no evidence that he received any legacies and if the money came from his legal fees he must have been a very successful lawyer. Since the 12,000 represented debts owed to Huet, perhaps he was merely a good debt-collector.

After 1789 he seems to have gone through a difficult period. He contracted an upholsterer's bill for 3,000 livres in August 1789 and still owed the money eighteen months later, when he secured an agreement to repay it in two instalments, in 1794 and 1796. In March and April 1791, however, he suddenly began investing in property, in or near his birthplace, on a large scale. Within less than a month he acquired land to the value of over 56,000 livres and a house that cost him another 25,000. This was a far cry from Bourdon's figure of 8–900,000, but it was still substantial. Moreover, Danton paid cash when, in the case of the land, which was former church property, he was only required to

57

put down twelve per cent of the purchase price and could have paid off the rest over a twelve-year period. This naturally set tongues wagging and Danton invariably replied that the money came from the reimbursement of his office. He did receive 69,000 livres in compensation – but he had just spent nearly 82,000. He paid for his house and land in March and April and in October had still not claimed the money owed him as compensation for his office. No evidence has come to light that he borrowed on the security of what was owing to him.

Disregarding the fact that Danton spent considerably more than he was due to receive, what he never explained was how, at the same time, he managed to pay off his considerable debts. The mortgage of 10,000 livres seems to have been liquidated before the suppression of the office itself and he made a final payment of 9,600 livres to Mlle Duhauttoir in August 1792. He also went on buying land at Arcis, on which he spent 27,000 livres in cash between the spring of 1791 and his death three years later. Looking at the period from his marriage to August 1792, this leaves an absolute minimum of about 60,000 livres unaccounted for, and probably a good deal more. It seems rather a lot to attribute to his legal prowess alone.

Danton's friend, Courtois, did his best. Writing in Danton's defence in August 1791, he claimed that when Danton wound up his legal practice he left unfinished business to the value of over 12 million livres.[4] That would indeed solve all the problems if only one could believe it. Courtois agreed that Danton had bought former church property to the value of 70–80,000 livres (the price he had actually paid for both the land and the house) but said Danton's father-in-law had put up half of the money – which was rather odd if Danton was doing as well as Courtois said he was. Courtois referred to the rumours that were already circulating about Danton's venality, including one that was to be particularly tenacious, to the effect that he was involved in forging paper-money. A former colleague of Danton's told Villiaumé that after Danton's office was suppressed he recovered debts to the value of 20,000 livres. This is a good deal more plausible than Courtois's 12 million; too plausible, in fact, to help, since it would still leave Danton at least 40,000 short. If he

4. *Lettre à l'auteur du Patriote Français*, p. 9 (Bibliothèque Nationale, Lb³⁹ 10160).

really was as successful a lawyer as his supporters have argued, which almost defies belief in view of his other commitments, and if his father-in-law helped him with his purchases, the accounts might just conceivably balance, but the probabilities are all the other way. Taking things at their face value, everything suggests that his financial situation took a dramatic turn for the better, for reasons that he was never able to explain, in the spring of 1791.

If one turns to the second line of approach – the testimony of Danton's associates – the evidence for Danton's venality is similarly plausible, but most of it falls just short of being wholly convincing. The son of one of his colleagues in the Convention, Cavaignac, set the general tone when he told Louis Blanc of a dinner party at which Danton, rather the worse for drink, said that the time had come for the revolutionaries to enjoy 'fine houses and food, handsome clothes and the women of their dreams', since the revolution was a battle and the spoils belonged to the victors. Faced with the disapproval of his fellow-guests, Danton assured them that he could play the sansculotte as well as anyone and *montrer mon derrière aux passants*.[5] It is all in keeping: the language, the profession of cynicism and Danton's version of the good life – but it is all third-hand stuff.

Some contemporary evidence is little more reliable. Madame Roland, whose contact with Danton allowed her to reinforce her political dislike of him with personal antipathy, said that he admitted to a fortune of $1\frac{1}{2}$ million livres. He may have said as much, to shock her, but if he did it was probably untrue. She noticed that he seemed suddenly to have come into money in 1789 but she did not accuse him of being paid by the court. Her political associate, Brissot, was more specific. He claimed to have actually seen a receipt from Danton to Montmorin, the Foreign Minister until May 1791, for 300,000 livres. This was pitching it rather high. Brissot does not seem to have repeated the charge in public and he was not the man to shrink from calumny when it suited his purpose.

The same figure, however, was mentioned by the Navy Minister, Moleville, in memoirs that first appeared in English in 1797. Moleville claimed that Talon, one of the court's agents for the distribution of secret funds, paid Danton more than 300,000 livres

5. Louis Blanc, *Histoire de la Révolution Française*, Book VIII, Chapter 1.

in return for his political services in the Jacobin club. He described how, on one occasion, he deterred his colleague, de Lessart, from paying Danton 24,000 livres for a single motion, which Moleville persuaded Dubois-Crancé to propose for nothing. At the time of the king's trial, at the end of 1792, Moleville said that he wrote to Danton, pretending to have written proof of his acceptance of money from the court and threatening him with exposure if he voted for the king's execution. He admitted in his memoirs that this was bluff, since although he had seen the receipt he did not have it in his possession. Whatever Danton may have thought of Moleville's threat – if he ever received it – it did not stop him voting for the king's death and Moleville's evidence does not add up to very much.

At the time of Danton's own trial one of his cousins wrote to the public prosecutor to say that Danton's wife had told him her husband had received 150,000 livres from the Lameths, the men who warned him to stay away from the Champ de Mars. It is quite possible, but well-timed revelations of this kind were such common currency that if one accepted them all there is not a revolutionary reputation that would be left intact.

La Fayette is a rather more convincing witness. He was a political opponent of Danton and he wrote his memoirs long afterwards but he was too honourable a man to invent defamatory charges or to repeat what he did not believe to be true – which does not mean that he was necessarily right. He claimed that he met Danton in Montmorin's office on the day that the minister arranged for Danton's legal office to be reimbursed at the price of 100,000 livres instead of the 10,000 that it had actually cost. This is the only transaction for which he claimed personal knowledge, though he referred elsewhere to Danton's receiving money after the Parisians' march to Versailles in October 1789, and another 150,000 livres just before the attack on the Tuileries on 10 August 1792. Unfortunately for La Fayette's evidence, Danton did not receive 100,000 livres for his office, but the more realistic figure of 69,000. He may, of course, have taken a bribe of 100,000 and disguised it as compensation for his office, but what La Fayette claimed as hard evidence turns out, on examination, to be as inconclusive as everything else.

In July and the first days of August 1792 rumours of attempts by the court to buy off the likely leaders of an insurrection flew thick and fast. Westermann, who was to lead the attack on the royal palace, claimed to have been offered 3 million by royalist agents who assured him that two of his acquaintances had already changed sides for the same price. Westermann said that he told Danton who called him a bloody fool for not reporting the matter to the police.[6] A royalist alleged that Danton's friend, Fabre d'Eglantine, asked for 3 million, but did not say whether or not he got it. La Fayette maintained that the king's sister, Madame Elisabeth, said to one of his acquaintances, 'We have nothing to worry about; we can rely on Danton'. Courtois, in his unpublished memoirs, asserted that Danton had a secret meeting with Marie Antoinette, without the king's knowledge, just before 10 August, at which he offered to protect her and her children. This might explain the misplaced confidence of Madame Elisabeth. If true, this proves nothing in particular. Danton could have been bought, or he may have been merely talking about the personal safety of the queen and her children – but not of the king – without offering to do anything to prevent the attack on the Tuileries.

All this is suggestive, and the regularity with which Danton's name keeps recurring is hardly likely to be a coincidence. At various times in his career he had the opportunity to destroy evidence that was better out of the way, and he may well have done so. All the same, one would have expected *something* to survive, when so many people claimed to have known so much, and there is, in fact, one piece of what looks like conclusive evidence. In the spring of 1791 Mirabeau, one of the agents of the court, was trying to control the subsidies handed out to its underground network. On 10 March he wrote a private letter to La Marck, his contact with the court, complaining that things were so badly organised that he was being attacked by men on the royal payroll. 'Beaumetz, Chapelier and d'André [three royalist deputies] dined yesterday *in secretis*, received the confidences of Danton etc. etc . . . Yesterday Danton got 30,000 livres and I have proof that he wrote the last number of Camille Desmoulins [in which Mirabeau had been violently attacked].'[7] Mirabeau was not making a public attack on Danton for political purposes

6. Archives Nationales, F[7] 4775[51].

7. *Correspondance entre le comte de Mirabeau et le comte de La Marck* (ed. A. de Bacourt), Paris, 1851, Vol. III, p. 82.

but casually citing him as an example of the poor value the court was getting for its money. He could have no motive for inventing a story that La Marck could easily verify for himself, and if Danton was not actually on the court's payroll the whole story was pointless. Even Robinet found this difficult to explain away and preferred to ignore it.

Putting together what has been discovered about Danton's finances and what was said about his venality, the case against him looks very convincing. At the end of 1789 he was suddenly in a position to repay debts that were not due until 1791. In March and April 1791 he bought a house and land to the value of over 80,000 livres and he had paid off his remaining debts by the following August. When called upon to explain where the money came from, he could only point to the 69,000 livres that he received for his office. The evidence of Moleville, La Fayette and Mirabeau all focuses on the spring of 1791, the precise time when Danton, who had been unable to repay his upholsterer at the end of January, suddenly embarked on his extensive purchases. Danton's venality has been responsible for the expenditure of much ink and acrimony but it is difficult to resist the conclusion that this is one historical controversy that need not go on for ever.

If Danton was paid, the question that immediately arises is what he did to earn his money and the answer is not at all clear. Mirabeau seemed to imply that he supplied the royalists with information about the tactics of their opponents, while Moleville said quite specifically that he was bribed to introduce or support motions in the Jacobin club. It does not seem much for what he got. Until the attack on the Tuileries, when his influence could have been important, he had not got much to sell. It is unlikely that he knew much more than an intelligent observer could have picked up from the public galleries of the Jacobins. He may, indeed, have regarded himself as a double agent, feeding the royalists with unimportant titbits about revolutionary tactics while trying to discover their own plans, which he could either use for his own purposes or pass on to the revolutionaries. Throughout his political life he was in his element in ambiguous situations of this kind where he could hope to persuade all the parties concerned that, whatever he had to pretend in public, he was secretly on their side. Like Mirabeau, he could tell the court that his more radical performances were merely designed to build up that popularity without which he could be of no use to them. The question of where his true allegiance lay, or whether he would not have been content with a reasonable position for himself after the victory of either side, is one that he may not even have asked himself. If one looks at him in this light, however, his behaviour in the spring of 1791 assumes a new perspective and the possibility arises that, beneath the ambivalence described in the previous chapter, there was yet another dimension.

His motions in the Jacobins did not give much away. Unlike almost all his contemporaries, he improvised his speeches and the only record that survives is what was noted in the press. The newspapers of the period concentrated on the National Assembly and many of Danton's interventions in the club may have gone unrecorded. Since he preferred to work through others, while remaining in the background himself, he may also have been responsible for more than he said himself. After attacking the ministers in May 1790 he is not recorded as having spoken again in the Jacobins before the beginning of 1791, when he challenged Mirabeau, who was in the chair, to get a hearing for Fabre d'Eglantine. He then became a good deal more vocal – just about the time when he was said to have been receiving money from the court. On 3 April he tacked on to a funeral oration in praise of Mirabeau the suggestion that the Constituent Assembly should wind itself up as quickly as possible and make way for its successor. Since the dead man had himself advocated the convocation of a new assembly, in the hope of strengthening the royalists, Danton was telling both the court and the radicals what they wanted to hear. He did it with such fervour that the club voted to petition for new elections within six weeks.

A fortnight later, on 18 April, Danton reported to the club the details of the royal family's unsuccessful attempt to leave for Saint-Cloud. The *Journal de la Révolution* gave the impression that he approved of the crowd's forcible intervention to keep the king in Paris, while the *Lendemain* said the opposite, which suggests that Danton was running true to form. In May and June he twice attacked royalist deputies, on issues that did not directly concern the royalist cause. Mirabeau had also struck up demagogic attitudes over unimportant issues, to cover his moderate stand on matters of substance and Danton may have taken him as his model.

When the king actually did escape, Danton concentrated his fire on La Fayette. This looked respectable enough, especially in retrospect, after La Fayette's men had fired on the crowd at the Champ de Mars. Robespierre and the hard core of the Jacobins were also bitterly opposed to La Fayette – and so was the court. Marie Antoinette was convinced that the Revolution was the work of ungrateful and disaffected nobles. The *canaille* whom they had stirred up could always be bought off or forcibly repressed, and the only opposition she took seriously was that which came from within the court circles she had known. She had a particular dislike of La Fayette, who had also been Mirabeau's *bête noire*. Once again, Danton's policy was sure to please almost everyone. It is difficult to know what to make of his proposals for the future of the monarchy, the *conseil à l'interdiction* and the 'sequestration of the vacant throne'. They were perhaps intended as holding operations that did not commit him to anything in particular and sounded threatening enough to reassure the Cordeliers while not being likely to lead to any practical results.

During the Champ de Mars crisis itself, in mid-July 1791, Danton was quite possibly playing for four or even five sides. He retained his position in the Jacobins while continuing to inspire the Cordeliers in their defiance of Jacobin caution. He may have had a hand in the Orleanist amendment to the Jacobin petition, to the effect that Louis should be replaced in accordance with the terms of the constitution (i.e. by his son, with Orleans as Regent). When he denounced monarchy in general and denied that the king was inviolable, on 13 July, he bellowed at the Jacobins, 'Let the National Assembly tremble!' This was good Cordelier stuff – but the court was unlikely to shed many tears if the Assembly did tremble. Danton was on good enough terms with the leaders of the Assembly he threatened for them to send him a personal warning to keep away from the Champ de Mars on 17 July. It was a virtuoso performance.

What gave Danton his opportunity was the fact that there were so many factions. If he attacked one – especially La Fayette, who was somewhat isolated – he could convince everyone else that he was on their side. In a situation of this kind it is very easy for the historian or the politician to suspect finesse and double-dealing where it may not have been present. It is quite possible that the Lameths and their followers were spoiling for a fight on the 17th and that the Cordeliers gave them the pretext they wanted. Robespierre suspected as much at the time and in 1794 he was to accuse Danton of deliberately playing their game for them. This looks a little hard. Danton may have been less of a clear-sighted manipulator than he was made to seem in 1794. He probably found the whole business as confusing as everyone else but he was certainly very good at tactical manoeuvring and convincing even those whom he seemed to oppose that he had a good deal in common with them.

His relationship with the Lameths is as obscure as everything else. When they tried to take over the rôle of the dead Mirabeau they may have inherited him as part of the goodwill of the business. Although they certainly warned him to steer clear of the Champ de Mars, Courtois accused them of spreading rumours about his venality. They must have been rather relieved to keep him out of the Legislative Assembly. After the summer of 1791 their own influence declined and Danton himself seems to have been off the stage in the autumn, perhaps looking after his new acquisitions in the Aube.

All the historians are agreed that the summer of 1792 was to be the most important period in Danton's career and it would be convenient if one could define his position as he approached the revolutionary climacteric. Unfortunately this does not seem to be possible. He was certainly a realist and a pragmatist. Unlike many of his contemporaries, he did not regard the Revolution as some kind of moral regeneration of France and humanity at large. To a man of his practical temper, the abstract principles he could vociferate in language that brought audiences to their feet were probably fairly meaningless – even if he himself was carried away at the time by the force of his own rhetoric. For him, democracy and republicanism were means rather than ends. What the ends were is obscure to us and may not have been very clear to Danton himself. Perhaps he was up for sale to the highest bidder or he may merely have taken money from anyone who was prepared to pay him, while continuing to go his own way – wherever that was. By 1792 he had made the coveted eighteenth-century transition from office to landed proprietorship. He could, at a pinch, afford to return to Arcis if the restoration of an effective monarchy wound up his political career. On the other hand, he may have been less of a cynic than he chose to pretend and prepared to risk a good deal to create a new kind of society that meant something to him.

If it will never be possible to say with confidence what Danton stood for, at least his political style emerges clearly enough. He was a professional politician of a new type, who combined a cool head for tactics with the kind of extrovert ebullience that won sympathy if not respect. Free from any sort of fanaticism, he could be ruthless in pursuing his ends, but he liked to be liked and he saw people as people and not as principles on two legs. He hated no one and was ready to co-operate with anyone and make the best of whatever turned up. He was unusual among the revolutionaries in his magnanimity towards those who were no longer dangerous. He was, by temperament, a political manager of a kind that is fairly common today, caught in a revolutionary situation where it was necessary to pretend that every issue was an apocalyptic battle between good and evil and every compromise was some sort of treason. He too could speak that kind of language when he had to, but he did it without much conviction. By 1792 he had proved himself to be a very skilful political operator; whether he was anything more and if so, whether he would get his chance to prove it, no one could tell.

V The Minister

By the end of 1791 the Revolution had reached stalemate. The king was unwilling to accept the new constitution and unable to challenge it. Most of the members of the Legislative Assembly, while genuinely devoted to the new order, were intent on compromise with a monarch who had no intention of compromising with them. They might grumble, criticise the ministers and vote for the repression of counter-revolutionaries, but in the last resort they accepted the royal veto and would not resign themselves to coercing the king. A radical minority which did not share their inhibitions was impatient to break this deadlock. Although these men did not form a party in the modern sense and always insisted on their political freedom of action, they formed an identifiable political group. Some of their most distinguished leaders had been elected to the Assembly by Bordeaux. They were eager to win a national reputation, eloquent in debate and characterised by a rather priggish provincial rectitude, a tendency to see politics in terms of abstract principles and an elevated sense of their own importance. It is because of them that the group as a whole is generally referred to as the Girondins, although contemporaries were more inclined to say Brissotins. As the latter name implies, the association had a Parisian element, very different from the provincials, consisting of men like Brissot who had lost their political innocence in the hard struggle for survival in the intellectual underworld of pre-revolutionary Paris. These men were similar in social background and experience to Danton's Cordeliers. Brissot's newspaper had been one of the very few to support Danton's campaign to get himself elected to the Legislative Assembly. Hitherto there had been nothing to distinguish them from the Cordeliers. Brissot had been a close friend of Marat before the Revolution and had been associated with Danton at the time of the king's flight. The two groups had criticised each other on occasion, there had been some journalistic duelling between Brissot and the touchy Desmoulins, and they had had their differences of opinion about the rival merits of Mirabeau and La Fayette. On the whole, however, they had all been part of a noisy radical movement, dissatisfied with what had emerged from the Revolution and convinced of the need for further changes.

Brissot now convinced himself that the way to break the political deadlock was by committing France to a limited war either against the minor German princes who were sheltering aristocratic opponents of the Revolution, or against their overlord, the Holy Roman Emperor. He believed that war would generate a new enthusiasm for the Revolution in France and force the king either to accept the new order and entrust the government to the war party, or reveal himself as the enemy of the nation – in which case he would presumably be overthrown. Brissot's calculations were to prove as accurate as most political projections, but he grossly under-estimated the dangers of war and over-rated the ability of the Girondins to handle any crisis they might provoke. The first consequence of his war policy was to split the radicals, with disastrous consequences for both the rival factions and for the future of the Revolution.

When the war campaign was launched in the Jacobin club in December 1791 it initially met with a favourable reception and attracted Robespierre's support. On 5 December, however, the Cordelier Billaud-Varenne sounded the alarm, pointing out that war was bound to increase the power of the suspect executive. Robespierre changed sides and on the 11th condemned the resort to war as a dangerous gamble. For the time being the issue was debated quietly and without recrimination. On 14 December Danton supported Robespierre's call for further debate, arguing that a war was likely to strengthen the hand of his old enemy, La Fayette, who had just been given command of one of the armies on the frontier. For the time being Danton did not have to choose. Gradually, however, the debate degenerated into a duel between Robespierre and Brissot in which the initial courtesies succumbed to the conviction of each that the other was, consciously or otherwise, playing the game of the court. Danton, who had at first praised Brissot personally, while supporting Robespierre, retorted somewhat sharply, at the end of the year, when Brissot accused his opponents of not respecting the constitution.

Early in 1792 the breach between the two sides became irreparable and the Jacobin club was paralysed by their conflict. The war party seems to have had the support of the majority, both within the club and amongst revolutionary opinion in general, and Robespierre wearied even his own supporters by repeatedly telling them about his unimpeachable revolutionary record. The Brissotin press insinuated that he had been bought by the court, a compliment that he returned in kind. As usual, Danton tried to avoid committing himself to either side. He made no more speeches about the war and confined himself to safe 'patriotic' subjects. Robespierre was later to accuse him of saying, 'If he [Robespierre] wants to destroy himself, let him; we mustn't share his fate'. Whatever the truth of that, at the time the relations between the two men remained cordial. Fabre d'Eglantine claimed that he tried to reconcile Robespierre and Brissot and, though he had no success, Robespierre acknowledged Danton's *patriotisme*.

For a time it looked as though Brissot had been right. On 23 March the king appointed three Girondin ministers, as a prelude to declaring war on Austria in the following month. Louis XVI had no confidence in his new ministers and no intention of following their advice, but the Girondins had obtained office, if not power. Danton's cultivation of both sides nearly won him the Ministry of Justice. His name was being bandied about in political circles towards the end of March, and on 3 April Desmoulins wrote to his father, 'For a couple of days I hoped to get Danton nominated, a school friend of mine [this was untrue] on the opposite side [presumably on the war issue] who thinks highly enough of me not to extend to my person his dislike of my views'. Danton himself maintained later that he had been offered the ministry by Dumouriez, the virtual prime minister, but had refused. This is not very likely. With some of their men in office, the Girondins now called for an end to destructive criticism and demanded national unity in support of the war. Their opponents replied by warning the troops to be on their guard against generals like La Fayette. It was not surprising that the campaign began badly, which naturally led each of the Jacobin factions to blame the other for the French reverses.

It may have been disappointed ambition that led Danton to move away from the Girondins and towards Robespierre. On 10 May he turned on them with one of those veiled hints of possible revelations that did so much to embitter personal relations between the revolutionaries: 'I am no agitator and for a long time I have maintained a painful silence . . . The time may soon come when one will have to denounce those who for the past three months have been attacking a reputation [Robespierre's] consecrated by the whole course of the Revolution.' Danton's friend and fellow-Cordelier, Robert, performed a similar evolution at the comic opera level; after publishing one or two attacks on Robespierre he claimed the Constantinople embassy as his reward. When the Girondins treated this as a bad joke Robert promptly rejoined their opponents.

When they discovered that the king had no intention of changing his policies the Girondin ministers became increasingly critical of him until he dismissed them on 12 June. This restored the precarious unity of the Jacobins who celebrated their new-found harmony by joining forces to attack La Fayette. This got no one very far, and as the advancing summer brought the threat of invasion by Austria's ally, Prussia, it looked as though France was heading for defeat and the restoration of royal authority by foreign arms. The question of what to do next split the Jacobins once again. The Girondins came to the mistaken conclusion that the king must have been intimidated by an armed invasion of his palace on 20 June and by rumours of a coming assault. Obsessed by the pursuit of office, they entered into secret negotiations with Louis in the hope that he would recall the three dismissed ministers. In the meantime they would oppose any attempt to overthrow him. Their opponents, after a good deal of hesitation, eventually steeled themselves to gamble on an insurrection.

Once again Danton found himself with the painful necessity for choice. By now there were only three sides left: the Girondins, their Jacobin opponents and the court. The Lamethists, whose policy of making the revolutionary compromise work had been wrecked by the war, had virtually disintegrated and nobody seemed to be thinking of Orleans. The day after the dismissal of the Girondin ministers, Danton had commended himself to both wings of the Jacobins by threatening to 'strike terror into a perverse court. The executive has only behaved with such audacity because we have been too weak.' On the following day he produced his detailed programme, which had at least the merit of originality. As proof of his militancy he began by recommending to his audience the law of Valerius Publicola which empowered any citizen to murder enemies of the state on his own initiative, provided that he subsequently produced the proof of their guilt.

This probably went down well with the public galleries but attracted no volunteers. His concrete proposals were for the more equitable assessment of taxation, which might very well strengthen support for the Revolution but would not stop many Prussians, and for a law that would oblige the king to repudiate Marie Antoinette and send her back to Austria. This would have been an excellent thing for all concerned if there had been the slightest prospect of its being voted by the Assembly or accepted by the king. Only a singularly naïve sansculotte could have taken Danton seriously. If he really did have a secret meeting with the queen soon afterwards, this suggestion must have made relations a little frosty, though no doubt Danton could have explained that it was all intended for the best. On 16 June he was rather more practical. After a ritual denunciation of La Fayette he supported a motion by Fabre d'Eglantine inviting the Paris Sections to draw up a petition to the Assembly. This was a polite way of urging them to put pressure on the deputies by mass agitation. As such, it could serve the Girondin policy of intimidation or help to raise the temperature in preparation for an insurrection.

Danton made only one speech between 16 June and the insurrection on 10 August. This related to the *fédérés*, National Guards sent up to Paris from the provinces to commemorate the taking of the Bastille and then make their way to reinforce the army at the front. The radicals hoped to use these militiamen for the coming attack on the Tuileries. Danton argued before the Jacobins that there would be nothing unconstitutional in the National Guards' swearing an oath at the Bastille celebration on 14 July 'not to leave Paris until liberty shall be securely established'. This was acceptable to both sides. His activities outside the Jacobins – at least his public ones – suggest that he accepted the need for an insurrection. Fabre, who seems to have been his contact man with Brissot, claimed at his trial that he tried to win Brissot to this point of view. Danton was not averse from a gamble, he had stronger nerves than Robespierre and he had perhaps done enough in the way of secret conversations with the court to be confident of saving his neck if things went badly. If they went well, there was no telling what might be possible. He was in the chair on 30 July when his Section voted to admit passive citizens (those disfranchised by their poverty) to its meetings and to service in the National Guard. This was the kind of popular motion, with overtones of direct democracy and popular sovereignty, that must have reminded him of the old days in the Cordelier District. By virtue of his position in the Commune, he was in touch with the central correspondence bureau of the Sections which co-ordinated their activities. When the 500 *fédérés* from Marseilles marched into Paris singing the song that was promptly named after them, Danton's colleague on the Commune, Panis, arranged for them to be billeted in the Cordelier club. The men from Brest had been quartered on the Cordeliers as soon as they arrived. Danton must have known all about the plans for the insurrection, in which Westermann was to play a leading part. He presumably hoped that it would succeed, but it would not have been out of character for him to insure himself against its failure.

One of the more militant Sections, Mauconseil, planned an attack on the Tuileries for 5 August. On the evening of the 4th another radical Section, Quinze-Vingts, had this attack postponed, to give the Assembly a chance to take action when it debated the state of the nation on the 9th. Quinze-Vingts served an ultimatum in due form, threatening to sound the tocsin at midnight on the 9th if it had not received satisfaction. Danton took advantage of the delay to pay a hurried visit to Arcis where he settled a small pension on his mother and another on his old nurse. Few of the revolutionaries would have thought of their elderly dependants at such a time. Apart from the light it throws on Danton's good nature, the little incident suggests that he expected to be fully committed in the coming crisis and was not sure that he had covered himself on all sides. He was back in Paris on the 9th. When the Assembly refused to impeach La Fayette, the tocsin punctually called the Sections to arms.

What Danton actually did has never been clearly established. At his trial he naturally claimed to have been at the centre of things.

I had prepared the 10th of August and I went to Arcis because Danton is a good son, to spend three days saying goodbye and winding up my affairs – there are witnesses. After that I was very much in evidence. It is not true that I went to bed. Although I was an official of the Commune I went to the Cordeliers. I told the minister, Clavière, who came from the Commune, that we were going to ring out the insurrection.

[Clavière did not, in fact, become minister until the Tuileries had fallen.] After arranging the plan of operations and the moment for the attack, I lay down on my bed like a soldier, with orders to call me. I left at one and made my way to the Commune like a revolutionary. I ordered the death of Mandat [the commander of the National Guard] who was in possession of an order to fire on the people. The mayor was arrested and I stayed at the Commune.[1]

Some of this is almost certainly exaggerated. The minutes of the Cordelier club contained no reference to Danton, though he may, of course, have made an unrecorded visit. He does not seem to have been concerned in the arrest of Mandat. Desmoulins's wife, Lucile, wrote an account of the night's alarms, towards the end of the year, which is dramatic but not very revealing. 'After dinner we all went to Danton's. His wife was crying and very depressed; her child looked stupefied. Danton was resolute. I laughed like a madwoman. They were afraid the affair would not take place.' The women went for a stroll in the street and when they returned they found Madame Robert and several others in the flat. When Desmoulins went out with his musket Lucile burst into tears and Camille tried to reassure her by promising to stay with Danton. Fréron said he was tired of life and only wanted to die. Danton left for the Hôtel de Ville. 'Danton came back to go to bed. He did not seem very keen and practically never left home. As midnight approached they came for him several times and he left at last for the Commune . . . Danton returned and threw himself on his bed.' Desmoulins returned at one o'clock and went to sleep on Lucile's shoulder. When dawn broke he went to bed.[2]

Lucile's account is tantalisingly inconclusive. She seems to imply that Danton was reluctant to involve himself in the preliminaries, on 9 August, but this could merely mean that he knew the Sections intended to overthrow the old Commune and realised that his presence at this stage might be merely an embarrassment to his allies. Nothing is known of what he actually did on the 10th – which has not prevented his admirers from attributing

1. Notes taken by Topino-Lebrun, reprinted in Robinet, *Danton, Homme d'Etat*, Paris, 1889, p. 451.
2. *Oeuvres de Camille Desmoulins* (ed. J. Claretie), Paris, 1874, Vol. II, pp. 198–9.

the leading rôle to him, or Mathiez from suggesting that he kept out of the way.

During the morning of the 10th the *fédérés* and the Parisian National Guards marched on the Tuileries which was only taken after heavy fighting in which hundreds of them were killed. The frightened Assembly suspended the king and voted for the election of a national Convention to take its place. Whatever his own share in the proceedings may have been, Danton was not the kind of man to miss the opportunities offered by the transformation of the political situation. Within twenty-four hours he had obtained the Ministry of Justice that had eluded him in the spring, securing the votes of 222 of the 284 deputies who still thought it safe to attend the Assembly. For the man who had had to try so many times before he won a minor place on the Paris Commune, this was indeed a triumph and it suggests that he was at least believed to have taken a leading part in the insurrection.

His election to ministerial office was arranged by Fabre and Brissot. According to the latter, Fabre told him that the *patriotes* wanted Danton to be minister and asked if Brissot had any objections. 'None at all. It must be the seal of our reconciliation.' Condorcet, who supported the Girondin group, explained their point of view. 'We needed a man who, by his oratory, his intelligence and his character would dishonour neither the ministry nor the deputies he would have to deal with. Danton alone possessed these qualities.' His election implied that he had succeeded in maintaining some sort of contact with the Girondins at a time when they and Robespierre had become open enemies.

However gratifying to his ambition and potentially lucrative, Danton's new position was an awkward one. The recent insurrection had been provoked by the refusal of the Assembly to dethrone the king and it had been opposed by most of the Girondins. Nevertheless the spoils of victory went, not to the insurgents, but to the Girondins. The new ministers, with the exception of Danton, were all their supporters and the flight of the constitutional monarchists from the Assembly left the Girondins in control of both the executive and the legislature. Real power in Paris itself, however, lay with the Sections and the new insurrectionary Commune. Understandably reluctant to accept the authority of those who had opposed the rising, the Commune was inclined to argue that the rump of the Assembly could no longer be regarded as the embodiment of national sovereignty, especially after the Assembly had voted its own demise. The Commune claimed not merely to represent the will of Paris but to anticipate the verdict of the country as a whole in the forthcoming elections. This may have been bad constitutional theory but it was a matter of revolutionary common sense: if the Assembly, or the electorate, wanted to restore the monarchy, Paris was not going to apologise for the insurrection and repair the damage to the Tuileries. In practice, the Commune did not seriously challenge the right of the Assembly to legislate on national matters but it aggressively asserted its own right to decide what happened in the capital, to have the royal family imprisoned and to punish those who had fired on the crowd on 10 August. The Girondins, who had previously acclaimed Paris as the stronghold of the Revolution, now began to denounce the city as the home of anarchy and to attack its spokesmen – notably Robespierre and Marat – as would-be dictators. Danton was not the man to put constitutional punctilio in the place of the realities of power, and all his political instincts must have urged him to try to reunite the republicans by bringing the Girondins to accept the temporary interregnum until the Convention could meet, and by urging moderation on the Commune. He was to learn that the price of power was the loss of his freedom of action. He had to reward his followers and his vigorous attempts to deal with the military crisis alienated the most dangerous of his ministerial colleagues.

As soon as he was installed in his new office, Danton began to pay off his political creditors – besides clearing his account with Mlle Duhauttoir. According to one story, Fabre d'Eglantine woke him up to tell him he had been made minister and in the same breath asked for the secretaryship of the ministry for himself. Danton split the post into two and gave half to Fabre and the other half to Desmoulins. Fabre also took advantage of the changed circumstances to obtain a contract to supply boots to the army. They were bad boots. Robert consoled himself for the loss of the Constantinople embassy by being put in charge of the ministry staff. Danton's old chief clerk, Paré, and his fellow-Cordelier, Billaud-Varenne, were found places on the Council of Justice. A third place was offered to Robespierre, who declined it. Paré soon exchanged his post for the secretaryship of the council of ministers. Danton treated his friends royally, in more senses than one. When the Commune and the Assembly sent emissaries all over the country to present the official version of what had happened on 10 August and act as propagandists for the new regime, the Cordeliers were not forgotten. Villain d'Aubigny, Panis, Dufourny, Momoro, Sentex, Ronsin, Vincent, Billaud, Legendre and Brune were all employed in this way. For several of them it was to be the beginning of a career and to awaken ambitions that would not be so cheaply satisfied in the future. Westermann and Fabre were sent on important missions to general Dumouriez when he halted the Prussian army of invasion in September. An obscure Parisian lawyer, Fouquier-Tinville, wrote to Desmoulins claiming to be a distant cousin and was found a place on the special court created to try those accused of planning the royalist 'attack' of 10 August.[3] For Fouquier too it was to be the beginning of a rather different career, as Danton and Desmoulins were to find to their cost. Danton had probably no illusions about the gratitude of those who inundated him with their professions of attachment. He is reported to have advised the young secretary of the Commune, Royer-Collard, about the time of the insurrection, 'Come and bawl with us. When you have made your fortune you will be able to take any side that suits you.'[4] He lived in the present and for the time being they could all be relied on to support their patron.

All this largesse did not escape the eye of Madame Roland, the thrustful wife of the Minister of the Interior. She aspired to create a new Roman republic in a France that seemed perhaps unworthy of the honour, resented Danton's ascendancy over his ministerial colleagues and found his coarse cynicism too un-Ciceronian for her taste. One has to beware of accepting her memoirs at their face value, since they were written with understandable venom while she was facing a mockery of a trial and she never understood how much her lofty refusal to accept Danton as a potential ally was responsible for her fate. She records how Danton invited himself to dinner, generally with Fabre d'Eglantine, almost every day until the end of August. She admitted his zeal,

3. Quoted in J. Claretie, *Camille Desmoulins, Lucile Desmoulins, Etude sur les Dantonistes*, Paris, 1875, p. 328 note 1.
4. Chateaubriand, *Mémoires d'outre-tombe* (ed. E. Biré), Paris, n.d., Vol. II, p. 28.

his devotion to the cause of liberty and his eagerness to co-operate with his Girondin colleagues, but convinced herself that a face like his must indicate 'the sway of brutal passions and the most extraordinary audacity half-concealed by an air of great joviality and the affection of frankness and a kind of good nature'.[5] It was not a bad character study, if she had left it at that, but she went on to describe him as a new Sardanapalus. Sexually frustrated in her marriage to a pompous civil servant much older than herself, she may have found Danton's celebrated masculinity rather uncomfortable. When he and Fabre suggested that Roland should subsidise a newspaper, to be written by Desmoulins and Robert, her austere Roman patriotism was unmoved by this touching solidarity of the quartet from the rue des Cordeliers. She accused Danton of being personally responsible for the selection of the agents sent into the provinces, 'a swarm of unknown men, intriguers from the Sections, bawlers of the clubs, *patriotes* out of fanaticism, and even more out of self-interest, most of them with no livelihood except what they hoped to pick up from political agitation, but devoted to Danton their protector and imitators of his licentious habits and doctrines'. Much of this was true, and Danton himself was not much of an asset to anyone's salon. There was little of the Jane Austen hero about him and his manners did not compare with those of Madame Roland's respectful admirers, but he was necessary and she was, after all, taking part in a revolution. When she turned her husband against him she was sealing the fate of all three of them.

Danton defined his position as Minister of Justice in a circular that he sent to all the courts of France on 19 August. As always, when he had just been elected to something, he put the emphasis on his moderation and claimed to stand for 'public and personal liberty, the maintenance of law and public order, national unity, the magnificence of the state and the prosperity of the people, not an impossible equality of wealth but equality of rights and happiness'. His survey of what had happened since 1789 was orthodox doctrine that Robespierre could have endorsed: the revolution of July 1789 had established the basis for the construction of a new society in accordance with the principles of Mably, Rousseau, Locke, Montesquieu and Franklin. (He did not

5.   *Mémoires* (ed. P. Faugère), Paris, 1864, vol. I, pp. 88, 97.

mention Adam Smith, although he owned a copy of the *Wealth of Nations*.) Unfortunately the electorate had tended to choose the old judges to fill the new courts set up by the revolutionaries and these conservative magistrates had been willing tools in the hands of counter-revolutionary ministers. What was needed now was not so much a new revolution as the honest implementation of the principles of 1789. The overthrow of the monarchy had made this possible and the courts would have to act in the new spirit. Where Danton parted company with many of the victors of 10 August was in his conciliatory attitude towards his old opponents. He was prepared to admit that the judges in the provinces had been misled by his ministerial predecessors and to offer them a new start. 'You can still win back the goodwill of the nation . . . turn against traitors and enemies of the public weal the sword of justice that [the monarchy] tried to turn, in your hands, against the apostles of liberty. Let the justice of the courts begin and the justice of the people will stop.' This was to repeat what he had said when sworn as minister on 11 August. He undertook then to protect the Assembly and called for an end to popular violence: 'When justice comes into action popular vengeance must cease.'

There can be little doubt that this is what Danton really wanted: the union of the revolutionaries behind the new government, an amnesty for anyone, whatever his past, who would either work with the new order or retire into private life, applause for the revolutionary Commune as the architect of regeneration, but its relegation to the routine administration of Paris. It was very reasonable, but it was not practicable. The Commune was bent on avenging the Parisian dead of 10 August and public opinion was increasingly alarmed by the threat of the approaching Prussian army. Robespierre's belief that compromise was impossible was a self-fulfilling prophecy. Under his leadership the Commune bullied the Assembly, which became increasingly resentful of Parisian pretensions. Danton might have to choose, in which case he could hardly be expected to desert the Jacobins and Cordeliers on whose support he depended.

In the meantime he was in his element. Alone amongst the ministers he showed himself capable of rising to the demands of a desperate situation. To their credit, all except Roland seem to have accepted his leadership, and his energy and resourcefulness earned him his statue just off the boulevard Saint-Germain. This was Danton's finest hour and he brought to it a Churchillian gusto. He was probably not exaggerating when he claimed later that, besides being Minister of Justice, he also acted as deputy Minister of War. He might have added that he was the right-hand man of the Foreign Minister as well. The fact that the men who kept an eye on Dumouriez's negotiations with the Prussians were Fabre, Westermann and Billaud-Varenne is a clear enough indication of who was giving the orders. Another group of his friends, Nöel, Danton's half-brother, Recordain and Mergez, were sent to England in the hope of preserving British neutrality, if necessary by the cession of Tobago. Informed by Chevetel, a neighbour from the Théâtre français, of plans for a rising in Brittany, Danton sent him to negotiate with the royalist leader, La Rouerie. He always preferred to deflect opposition rather than to meet it head on and he was indifferent to his own reputation, so he seems to have given La Rouerie the impression that he himself was a royalist sympathiser. He probably thought this would do no harm and might win precious time. When Mathiez came across the correspondence, he at least took Danton's bait and pronounced him a crypto-royalist.[6] With Danton all things are possible and this could just have been another of his insurance policies, but after 10 August he could not have had much to hope for from the Bourbons.

The most pressing danger came from the Prussians who crossed the frontier in mid-August, took the forts of Longwy and Verdun, which should have held them off until the end of the campaigning season, and began their march on Paris. Everything that seemed to have been won was now in jeopardy. If one can believe Fabre d'Eglantine, Roland proposed that the government should leave Paris to its fate and withdraw to Blois with the king. Servan (War) and Clavière (Finance) agreed with him. Danton put a brutal stop to this by telling them that he had just brought his mother and his children to Paris and would see it burned down rather than let in the Prussians. He apparently advised Roland not to talk too loudly about flight in case the Parisians heard him — which cannot have endeared him to either the Minister of the Interior or his wife.

6.   A. Mathiez, *Danton et la Paix,* Paris, n.d., Ch. 2.

On 25 August the government issued a proclamation to the nation which reads as though Danton drafted it. No attempt was made to disguise the seriousness of the military situation.

Generous citizens, all we ask of you is to be true to yourselves. We shall not try to conceal from brave men all the risks and sacrifices that your new enterprise involves. The French people are already confronting the kings; the terrible collision has already begun and in this battle – which deserves the attention of the whole world – the only choice is between victory and death. Citizens, no nation on earth ever won its freedom without a fight. You have traitors in your midst; without them the struggle would soon be over. Keep united and calm. Plan your means of defence wisely and execute them with courage and victory is assured.

The men of the Commune were more responsive to talk of treason than of wisdom. Absurd rumours were already circulating of a royalist plot to open the prisons and use their inmates to hold Paris until the Prussians should arrive. Encouraged by Marat, who thought the solution to most problems began with the massacre of as many of one's opponents as possible, one or two Sections were already calling for the murder of the common criminals and political prisoners with whom the gaols were crowded. This was not Danton's way of doing things. On the other hand, the country was unlikely to survive the military crisis if its enthusiasm was not aroused, and the more he stressed the danger and sounded the call to arms, the more likely it was that the prisoners would suffer. The most probable explanation of his attitude at the end of August is that he pursued national defence at any cost, that he realised what the cost would be and accepted it. The alternative explanation, that the prison massacres were an act of deliberate policy on his part, though not entirely ruled out by the evidence, is less likely. Once they had happened, he not merely refused to condemn them – which would have meant repudiating Paris – but claimed that they were his work. The Girondins could scarcely be blamed if they took him at his word.

Towards the end of August the Commune, which had already told the Assembly that deputies were applying for passports under false names, closed the gates of Paris to prevent suspects escaping.

On the 28th Danton came to the Assembly with a rather ambiguous speech. He began on a note of reassurance. 'Our enemies have taken Longwy but Longwy is not France. Our armies are still intact.' He went on to call for a great popular effort to throw the Prussians back.

> The time has come to tell the people that they must throw themselves upon their enemies *en masse*. When a ship is wrecked the crew throws overboard everything that endangers it. In the same way, everything that might endanger the Nation must be expelled and whatever may be of use put at the disposal of the local authorities, in return for compensation.

He therefore proposed the levy of all men fit to go to the front, together with household searches to discover arms that could be requisitioned and to arrest suspects. 'If we have to place 30,000 traitors in the hands of the law, let us do it tomorrow, but let us open up communications with the rest of France.'

His main aim was probably to conciliate the Commune and to rouse Paris by a gesture of military defiance. There was no prospect of the volunteers being ready for action in time to stop the Prussians before winter put an end to the fighting, but the knowledge that they were coming might have a decisive effect on the morale of the rest of the army. His call to arms was repeated in the most famous of all his speeches, delivered on 2 September, the day fixed by the Commune for the enlistment of volunteers. This was a fighting speech in every sense of the word, and its peroration, delivered with the full force of his formidable lungs, has echoed down history.

> The tocsin that will ring is no signal of alarm; it is sounding the charge against the enemies of the nation. *Pour les vaincre, Messieurs, il nous faut de l'audace, encore de l'audace, toujours de l'audace et la France est sauvée!*

It was magnificent and it worked, but – with Danton there is always a 'but' – the dramatic household searches going on through the night both terrified opponents and exacerbated the strain on Parisian nerves, besides yielding more suspects than muskets and concentrating attention on the bulging gaols. Fréron and Fabre, who were two of Danton's close friends, were advocating an attack on the prisons in the newspapers. In both his speeches Danton had referred to the need for violent action against the 'enemies of the nation' as well as the Prussians, and he knew that, for the Commune at least, counter-revolution began at home. The tocsin that called the Parisians to volunteer also seems to have served as a signal for the massacre of the prisoners and Danton was generally well informed about what was going on. Two members of the Commune's *comité de surveillance*, which organised the butchery, if anyone did, were his old colleagues, Panis and Sergent. During the previous few days the Assembly had wearied of the Commune's hectoring and ordered new elections. Mortimer-Ternaux claimed – though without producing any evidence – that the Girondins intended to dismiss Danton at the same time.[7] It is not difficult to see all this as confronting Danton with a choice between Commune and Assembly, with the former intent on a bloodbath that would intimidate the deputies – and also those Parisians who, on 2 September, were beginning the process of choosing their representatives to the Convention. In a conversation in the autumn with the Duc de Chartres (the future King Louis-Philippe), Danton put forward another argument for the massacres. 'Do you know who organised those September massacres about which you rant so violently and irresponsibly? I did . . . I wanted the youth of Paris to reach Champagne covered with the blood that would assure us of its loyalty; I wanted to put a river of blood between them and the *émigrés*.'[8] Danton also said to Chartres: 'It often happens, especially in time of revolution, that one has to applaud actions one would not have wanted or dared to perform one's self'. Applying the second remark to the first is a reminder that Danton's unsupported word can never be taken as evidence, not even against himself.

Whether he planned the massacres or made no attempt to stop others from doing so, once they had started he behaved like the rest. Both the Assembly and the Commune tried to reason with the murderers but no one was prepared to try to stop them by force. That would have required the mobilisation of the National Guard, which might well have refused to open fire, or another Champ de Mars affair that would have put paid to any hopes of persuading the Parisians to leave for the front, as 20,000 did within the first weeks of September. According to Madame

7. *Histoire de la Terreur*, Paris, 1862–9, Vol. II, p. 132.
8. Louis-Philippe, *Mémoires*, Paris, 1973, p. 224.

Roland, when Danton was leaving the council of ministers on the afternoon of 2 September, Grandpré, the inspector of prisons, told him of his concern for those in his care. 'I don't give a damn for the prisoners,' replied Danton, 'let them look after themselves as best they can.' Her own friends were less open about it but they remained inactive and her husband even described the slaughter, in an official circular, as 'a kind of justice'.

The massacres threatened to spread from Paris to the rest of the country. Particularly vulnerable were the state prisoners awaiting trial before the High Court at Orleans. On 24 August the Commune, on the pretext of a royalist plot, detached a force of 500 men under the Cordelier, Fournier, to Orleans. Danton seems to have supported the attempts of the Assembly to get the prisoners transferred to Saumur, out of harm's way, but the Parisians insisted on bringing them back. When they reached Versailles the president of the criminal court there, Alquier, came to tell Danton of his fears for the prisoners' safety. Danton told him it was no business of his and refused to intervene. On 9 September they were massacred by their escort.[9]

Whatever Danton's attitude may have been, and it looks as though he hoped to avoid the massacres but was not prepared to forfeit his revolutionary reputation in an attempt to stop them, at least he did not use them to get rid of his opponents. Both Robespierre and Billaud-Varenne, just before the massacres began, denounced the leading Girondins as agents of Brunswick, the Prussian commander-in-chief. When the slaughter had actually started, a warrant was issued for the arrest of Roland, but Danton tore it up.[10] He intervened personally to save Charles de Lameth, arrested in Normandy, and Lameth's old associate, Duport. Danton prevented Duport's being brought to Paris for trial, despite the efforts of Fabre d'Eglantine, who leaked information to the comité de surveillance. This led to a violent quarrel between Danton and Marat in which Danton more than held his own. Some of the men he helped to get out of Paris, such as Talon, a former distributor of royal largesse, were perhaps better out of the country, from Danton's point of view. His detractors have

9. Mortimer-Ternaux, *Histoire de la Terreur*, Paris, 1862–9, vol. II, pp. 359–400.

10. Mortimer-Ternaux (vol. III, p. 139) refers to arrest warrants for Brissot, Roland and thirty deputies.

argued that he saved Duport from similar motives of self-preservation. But one of the men murdered at Versailles, de Lessart, also knew of Danton's dealings with the court and it seems a little hard to accuse him of saving the one and conniving at the death of the other from the same motive.

When the Convention met, in the second half of September, the Girondins were to use the massacres to brand Paris as the home of anarchy and its deputies as men of blood. One can understand their feelings, especially after the efforts of Robespierre and Billaud to include them among the victims; and Danton's insistence, not merely on the inevitability of the massacres but on his own responsibility for them, put him in the enemy camp. He probably thought they would get over it. He himself was used to accepting the realities of politics and the need to subordinate personal feelings to the demands of the tactical situation, and he perhaps under-estimated the implacability of the Rolands and the ostentatious rectitude of their friends. It was bitterly ironical that the August crisis, the one occasion when he was able to prove himself as a national statesman rather than a mere party manager, should have forced him into the kind of choices he was normally so successful in avoiding. The man who seemed made to preside over a united republican movement in the Convention was to find himself the prisoner of its dissensions, helpless to prevent a savage faction fight that was alien to his whole conception of politics, to whose fatal consequences the Girondins were blind and he was not.

VI The Deputy

While the unfortunate prisoners were being slaughtered, Paris was electing its twenty-four deputies to a national Convention.[1] The Legislative Assembly had been so afraid of seeming to infringe popular sovereignty that it had not felt qualified to do more than *suggest* the manner in which the elections should be conducted and the date on which they should be held. This was all very well, but the actual choice of the electorate was inevitably circumscribed. It was unrealistic to assume that those who had won the battle of the Tuileries at such heavy cost would accept a verdict that reversed the situation and put the king back on the throne. The result was a good deal of electoral 'guidance' which took different forms in different parts of the country but secured the election of an overwhelmingly republican assembly. In the case of Paris, one can catch glimpses of the intervention of leading politicians, the Jacobin club, the Commune and some of the Sections. This was clearly a situation in which Danton's Cordelier machine could exercise an influence out of all proportion to its numbers.

Robespierre persuaded his own Section to opt for public and indirect elections, with the electors for the city as a whole meeting at the Jacobin club and the results being subject to the confirmation of the Sections. The Commune, which had fewer inhibitions than the Legislative Assembly about prescribing rules to the sovereign people, ordered the general application of this procedure throughout Paris. The Jacobins, at first reluctant to suspend their own business, were persuaded by Robespierre and Collot to allow their hall to be used by the electors. The latter numbered about 990, of whom 850 came from Paris itself and the remainder from the surrounding country districts. Since the previous elections, only a year before, 80 per cent of the electors were new. Danton's own Section, which had altered its name from Théâtre

1. P. Mautouchet, 'Le mouvement électoral à Paris en août-septembre 1792', *Révolution française*, 1903, and Alison Patrick, *The Men of the First French Republic*, Baltimore, 1972, pp. 139–293. I am happy to have this opportunity of thanking Mrs Patrick for her advice about the Paris elections.

français to Marseille, to commemorate its billeting of the men from the south who had led the attack on the Tuileries, was probably unique in changing less than half of its previous electors. On 3 September Collot denounced those electors who had previously belonged to conservative clubs or signed monarchist petitions, and Robespierre persuaded the meeting to order them to be replaced. This ensured a republican majority but it was still necessary to convert those who might vote for Girondins, rather than for the men from the Commune. Rival lists were circulating in the press, notably in the newspapers of Marat and Louvet. Robespierre and Danton were two of the few names that appeared on both. In a speech to the electors, Collot denounced

> men too easily persuaded that they are superior beings, men who isolate themselves in their offices and, proclaiming themselves our masters, only too often do all they can to become our masters in fact . . . They are not our masters; our revolutionary masters are those who raised the faubourgs on the 10th of August and marched in their van.

This was an invitation to substitute a new political generation, the men of the Commune and the Cordeliers, for the gentlemen of 1791 and their Girondin leaders.

On 5 September Robespierre became the first man elected, polling 338 votes out of 525. Many of the electors had still to arrive, and Pétion, the Girondin mayor of Paris, attracted 136 votes, which accounts for the low poll and Robespierre's apparently poor showing. Pétion, hearing of his election in the provinces, conceded defeat in Paris and withdrew. On the following day Danton received 638 votes out of 701, over 90 per cent of the poll and one of the highest majorities that was to be recorded. He decisively beat Collot although the latter was in the chair and seems to have been managing proceedings. For the man who had been so consistently ostracised by the Parisian electorate, this must have been particularly gratifying. How far it meant a change in people's opinions about him and how far it merely reflected a purge of the electorate, it is impossible to say. Danton's influence over the remaining elections is difficult to judge, but when Desmoulins came under heavy criticism on the 8th, Danton defended him and ensured his election. He and the Cordeliers were also credited with the choice for the last of the twenty-four places of Orleans, who rather reluctantly agreed to accept the absurd name of Philippe Egalité.

The result of the Parisian election was a triumph for the men of 10 August in general and for the Cordeliers in particular. With twenty-four deputies representing forty-eight Sections, the Cordeliers and the Section Marseille could not reasonably have expected to win more than the odd seat. They gained ten. Danton himself and the friends and neighbours who were his closest political allies, Fabre d'Eglantine, Desmoulins, Robert and Legendre, were all returned, together with Billaud, Collot, Fréron and Marat. Henceforth the deputies from Paris, sitting on the highest benches in the Convention, were to form the nucleus of a group known as Montagnards. From the beginning they behaved as part of the new revolutionary Establishment. No doubt they retained some of the habits they had acquired in their old days as street politicians, but henceforth they saw themselves as national legislators working through the Assembly.

Danton had done well for his lieutenants, but there is never enough political patronage to go round. Hébert, a recent Cordelier, the author of a newspaper, *Le Père Duchesne*, that was acquiring a radical tone and the vernacular language of the Parisian working man, had replaced Danton on the Commune. During several rounds of the election to the Convention he had stood as a candidate, but never obtained more than half a dozen votes. Ronsin, another Cordelier and apparently a friend of Danton, had asked Robespierre for support, but fared no better. Henceforth these two and other Cordeliers such as Vincent, Chaumette and Momoro, took over the club which Danton and the more fortunate members had deserted for the Convention and the Jacobins. They also took over Cordelier tactics and attitudes: suspicion of the government, the reckless denunciation of their opponents and the threat of violence from the streets. Unlike the old Cordeliers, who had never had any other source of power, their successors dominated the Commune and were soon to extend their empire to the War Office, but always as men dissatisfied, whose aspirations demanded a new 10 August and a third revolution.

Despite the financial attractions, legitimate and otherwise, of his ministerial office, on the day the Convention met, Danton resigned it, since he could not be both minister and deputy. He agreed to remain in office until a successor could be appointed.

True to form, he welcomed his election to the Convention with a profession of moderation. He concluded his speech of resignation:

> Until now the people has been agitated because one had to awaken it against its tyrants. From now onwards the law must be as terrible against those who infringe it as the people have been in pulverising tyranny . . . People seem to think, excellent citizens may have been led to believe, that passionate friends of liberty might harm the social order by the exaggeration of their principles. Let us renounce all exaggeration and declare a perpetual guarantee of every kind of property: landed, personal and industrial.

All his proposals were voted by the Assembly. For the time being he seemed popular with almost everyone. The Convention invited him to remain at the Ministry of Justice, the Jacobins elected him their president, the Girondin journalists, Condorcet and Gorsas, praised him, Vergniaud, the foremost Girondin orator, was well-disposed towards him and all the ministers except one accepted his lead. Until his replacement by Garat on 11 October he was still the leading figure on the ministerial council. The only personal opposition came from Madame Roland and her husband and probably reflected hurt vanity as much as anything else. Danton was curiously sensitive to this. On 29 September when the Assembly was discussing whether to invite him and Roland to remain at their posts, he offended the deputies with the sarcastic suggestion that the invitation be extended to Madame Roland as well, 'for everyone knows that Roland was not alone in his office. I was alone in mine.' It was not a wise thing to say and it was not in character. Danton was not a touchy man and though he probably found Madame Roland's Roman posturing something of a trial, he would not normally have allowed his feelings to lead him into a blunder of this kind. He was probably exasperated by the fact that Madame Roland's entourage was succeeding in dividing the Assembly by its repeated attacks on the Parisians, their deputies, and Marat, Robespierre and Danton in particular, as anarchists soaked in the blood of September. Whether his main concern was with his own position or with the disinterested pursuit of republican unity, the situation was equally unfortunate.

On 25 September a Girondin attack on the Parisian deputation, as would-be dictators, still found him in a conciliatory mood. He began by disclaiming any responsibility for the views of his twenty-three colleagues, went on to dissociate himself from Marat and won general support for his proposal to vote the death penalty both against those who proposed a dictatorship and those who advocated a federal constitution (a charge the Montagnards threw against the Girondins). On the 28th he advocated exporting the revolution: 'We have the right to say to [foreign] peoples: you will have no more kings . . . The Convention must be a general insurrectionary committee against all the kings of the universe.' He did not believe it and it bore no relationship to the actual foreign policy he was conducting in secret, but he may have thought that it would appeal to men like Brissot who had a weakness for that kind of language.

It was singularly embarrassing for Danton, and very convenient for those determined to reject any political compromise, when he came under personal attack from an entirely new quarter. A businessman from Montpellier, Cambon, had scarcely taken his seat in the Convention before he made himself the watchdog of the financial interests of the republic. Danton had already disagreed with him on 27 September, when Cambon wanted to reduce priests' salaries. On 10 October Cambon drew attention to the unsatisfactory way in which the ministers had handled the credit of 2 million livres, half for 'extraordinary' and half for secret expenses, voted them on 28 August. Instead of assuming collective responsibility for the money, the total had been divided up amongst the different ministers and Cambon was sceptical about the justification for secret expenditure by Justice, the Navy, the Interior and Taxation. Some of the ministers had spent nothing, or very little. Of the total expenditure of over 400,000 livres, most had been incurred by the Minister of Justice.[2] Cambon therefore proposed to annul the vote of 2 million and invite the ministers to account for the sums actually spent. Danton, never short of nerve, seconded this motion and praised Cambon, but added that he himself had already rendered his accounts. He explained the extent of his expenditure by the fact that he had been 'as much the adjutant-general of the War Minister as Minister of Justice'.

2. On this obscure question see A. Mathierz, *La corruption parlementaire sous la Terreur*, Paris, 1917, pp. 70–97.

On 18 October Roland rather ostentatiously accounted for every penny of his own expenses. The Girondin, Rebecqui, then demanded that the other ministers follow suit. Monge, for the Navy, said he had spent nothing – which perhaps helps to account for the lamentable condition of the fleet. Danton was well-received when he began with the argument that it had been more important to make sure of victory than to count the pennies, but the deputies were rather less happy when he spelt out the implications of his patriotic doctrine: 'You wanted the ministers to act in concert. We did so and that constitutes our accounts.' Danton rested his case on the fact that his 'accounts' had been accepted at a meeting attended by all the ministers except Roland. When Cambon criticised Roland for this evasion of his responsibility, Roland replied that he had tried to verify the accounts but the registers were missing. Danton pointed out that secret expenditure was never recorded on the registers but could say nothing about the 'extraordinary' expenditure, which should have been. Since Danton was covered by all the ministers except Roland there was nothing the Assembly could do, but the question festered for the next six months. Whenever the Girondins wanted to embarrass or discredit Danton they shouted 'the accounts!' This was a useful threat to keep in reserve – they never seriously tried to expel him from the Assembly – and a useful reminder of the general turpitude of the Paris deputation.

The fight went on all through the autumn, with the Girondins on the offensive all the time. On 29 October Roland proposed to send to the provinces a circular denouncing anarchy in Paris. This naturally set off another battle between the two factions, in which Danton once again disowned Marat and claimed to be 'without party and without faction'. He went out of his way to acknowledge Roland's 'passionate love of order and legality' which he said explained the minister's tendency to see a vast conspiracy behind every minor riot or petty crime. Considering what he had had to put up with, Danton was remarkably conciliatory. He agreed that some people might have profited from the breakdown of order to pursue acts of private vengeance, but invited his audience to put things in perspective. 'No throne was ever shattered without some worthy citizens being hurt by the splinters.' There can be no doubt about Danton's sincerity in appealing for Girondin co-operation. It had no effect. Louvet, a habitué of the Rolands' salon, replied

with a diatribe against Robespierre and Marat that included occasional aspersions against Danton. When Robespierre defended
himself on 5 November, he too called for an end to party bicker-
ing, but with no more success. In view of the determination of
some of the Girondins to attack the Montagnards at any price,
Danton would have found it very difficult to hold the Convention
together, even if he had not been suspected of corruption. He
would, however, have been able to risk an appeal to the rank and
file of both groups, over the heads of their leaders. As it was,
he needed the protection of the Montagnards, which limited his
independence. On 30 October the ministers were once again
instructed to present detailed accounts. When, on 5 November,
they said that Danton and the War Minister, Servan, had done
so, Brissot demanded that Danton justify himself in public and
Cambon accused him of still having money for which he had not
accounted.

Danton continued on his way, as the man who had explained
all and had nothing to hide. On the religious question he showed
more good sense than the penny-wise Cambon and the high-
principled Girondins. When rioting broke out in the Eure-et-Loir,
reports stressed peasant anger at rumours that the Assembly was
about to stop paying priests. This furnished the Girondin,
Birotteau, with the text for a sermon on popular superstition.
Danton's view was rather different. He said the peasants had
been misled by mistaken or evilly-intentioned commentaries on
Cambon's original motion. In fact, Cambon had merely suggested
lowering salaries and it was Danton's friend, Delacroix, who had
proposed abolishing them, but Danton had had to put up with
rather a lot from Cambon and this was too good an opportunity
to be missed. Danton professed his own philosophical deism, 'I
recognise only the god of the universe, only the cult of justice
and liberty', but stressed that the unfortunate needed stronger
consolation.

> The man abused by fortune looks for bliss elsewhere. When
> he sees the rich gratify all their tastes and indulge all their
> desires, while his own requirements are restricted to the barest
> necessities, he believes, and his consolation comes from his
> conviction, that his bliss in the next world will be proportionate
> to his privations in this one. Leave him with this error of his.

Wait to speak to him of morals and philosophy until he has been enlightened by persuasion and can appreciate religious opinions at their true value . . . Until then it is treason to the nation to want to deprive the people of its ideas and its fancies.

These were the accents Robespierre was to use – with Danton's support – just a year later, and Danton's position now was like Robespierre's then. Each was trying unsuccessfully to unite the Convention, torn between a moderate faction impatient for the end of the revolution and an extremist one intent on carrying it further. Robespierre's suspicion of the Girondins helped to frustrate Danton in 1792 and Danton's allies were to foil Robespierre in the following year. Most of them were to pay for it with their lives.

During this period Danton had also been busy behind the scenes. So far as one can judge, he shared the view of most of the Girondins that France's real enemy was Austria and that other actual or potential opponents could be bought off or neutralised. England was to be offered Tobago in return for neutrality and a loan. The negotiations with Prussia after the Prussian army had been halted at Valmy have never been fully elucidated. The King of Prussia was anxious to extricate his disease-ridden troops from France without further fighting and he had every incentive to talk his way to safety by inconclusive negotiations. Dumouriez, the French commander-in-chief, was eager to transfer his forces to the north, to clear the Austrians out of Belgium, and disinclined to continue the campaign against the Prussians. This is perhaps enough to explain why the Prussian army was allowed to retreat unmolested. Contemporaries thought otherwise and sniffed treason, as they usually did. Danton's remark, on 18 October, that if the ministers had spent another 10 million not a single Prussian would have escaped from France, may simply have been part of his general defence of secret expenditure. If it meant anything more, it suggested that something had been paid to someone. With Fabre, Westermann and Benoît as middlemen, a fair amount no doubt disappeared in transit. Brunswick, the Prussian commander, is said to have returned to Germany mysteriously free from his considerable debts. Whatever actually happened, it looks as though Danton was under the impression that he was buying off the Prussians. Frederick William, their king, may have been equally convinced that he had fooled the French. When the military situation improved and the revolutionaries became over-confident, it seemed to many of them that the Prussians had been allowed to escape.

Danton's actual policy of limiting the war to Austria was in direct contrast to the attitudes he struck in the Convention, where he asserted the French right to occupy Geneva, called for the incorporation of Savoy and demanded a debate on the desirability of declaring war on Spain. He was always willing to tell an audience what it wanted to hear and, whatever he thought of the merits of educating the peasantry in the principles of deism, he preferred to leave his colleagues in happy ignorance of the implications of the balance of power. Whatever allowance one makes for the pressure of circumstances, it is difficult to acquit him of reckless irresponsibility. When he demanded the annexation of Belgium on 31 January 1793 he must have known that this would make war with England inevitable. He may have thought it inevitable in any case, but the expansionist policies he encouraged were to plague him when he became responsible for French foreign policy.

Danton preferred meeting people to putting things on paper, which does not make things easier for his biographers. Traces have survived of two such meetings in the autumn of 1792. One of these was with the Duc de Chartres. Although only nineteen, Chartres commanded his family regiment and the massive desertion of army officers meant that he was one of the senior French generals at the battles of Valmy, Jemappes and Neerwinden. As the son of Philippe Egalité, he was naturally associated with the perennial rumours of an Orleanist plot, with which Danton's name, too, was linked. When garbled accounts of Danton's interview with Chartres leaked out in the nineteenth century, his rôle as an Orleanist agent seemed to be confirmed. The only record of what happened comes from Chartres himself and the full version, which only became available in 1973, conveys a different impression. The future Louis-Philippe, writing long after the event, said that he attended a meeting of the council of ministers at which Danton took him to one side, saying, 'Don't waste your time talking to that idiot [Servan, the Minister of War]. Come and see me tomorrow.' At the private meeting on the following day Danton advised Chartres to stop denouncing the September massacres, for which he claimed responsibility. 'You make me shudder, Monsieur Danton.' 'Shudder as much as you like, but learn not to keep on shuddering in public. That's the best advice I can give you.' As Chartres presents the story, Danton, far from seeking to ingratiate himself, tried to impress the future king with his ruthlessness and to frighten him into keeping his distance from the Girondins, who might benefit from his popularity, by insinuating that this might endanger his father, who was one of the less distinguished of the Montagnards.[3] That sounds plausible enough. Of course, if Danton did take a rather more friendly interest in Chartres, which would have been quite sensible since he would have made a much better constitutional monarch than his father, Louis-Philippe might have preferred to draw a veil over that, when he was king and Danton a long-dead monster. One can scarcely assume, though, that the evidence means the exact opposite of what it purports to say, and, for what the record is worth, it confirms Danton's Montagnard credentials.

The second interview was potentially more compromising. Théodore Lameth, one of the constitutional monarchists who had tried to arrange a compromise with the king and had warned Danton to keep away from the Champ de Mars on 17 July 1791, after escaping to England, returned to Paris in October 1792 in the hope of saving the king's life. As a returned émigré, he was liable to execution if caught. This did not prevent him from appearing before Danton and trying to enlist his support. His long verbatim account of their conversation can scarcely be literally exact and there is no means of knowing how far it is distorted.[4] According to Lameth, Danton said: 'We must pass through rotten democracy [la sale démocratie] in order to reach liberty'. Lameth defended the king's part in the Revolution, without making much of an impression on Danton. He then urged him to rescue Louis XVI or procure the means for his escape. Danton replied that the king's death seemed to him neither just nor expedient and promised to do what he could to avert a trial that could have only one outcome. 'But if I have to give up all hope, I warn you that, since I don't want my head to fall with his, I shall join those who condemn him.' In a second interview,

3. Louis-Philippe, *Mémoires*, Paris, 1973, pp. 218–25.
4. Text in A. Mathiez, *Danton et la paix*, Paris, 1919, pp. 68–71.

Danton told Lameth that he and Delacroix were already working on plans to save the king.

There is nothing very surprising about this and it is scarcely proof that Danton was a crypto-royalist. He probably told Lameth only as much as he intended him to know and his policy with regard to the monarchy may have been rather more complicated. The American ambassador, Gouverneur Morris, wrote to Jefferson on 21 December 1792; 'Shortly after the 10th of August I had information, on which you may rely, that the plan of Danton was to obtain the resignation of the king, to get himself appointed Chief of a Council of Regency, composed of his creatures, during the minority of the dauphin. This idea has never, I believe, been wholly abandoned.'[5] Diplomats usually think their sources of information well-informed and it would be unwise to read too much into that. It could be true, since Danton probably had little faith in the *mystique* of a republic and was relatively indifferent to the form of government, provided that the essential gains of the Revolution (whatever he thought those to be) were preserved. He was always generous towards defeated opponents and it may have seemed to him good policy to trade the king's life against the neutrality of Spain, and perhaps of England as well. If he did anything at all it would have to be secretly since the hostility of the Girondins and the temper of public opinion meant that it would be political suicide for him to present the case for clemency to the Convention. Given his reputation, any such approach would be universally taken as proof that he had been bribed. Secret action meant bribing other deputies and would cost a great deal of money. The Montagnard deputy, Chabot, was reported to have received 2 million livres from the Spanish ambassador and Théodore Lameth claimed that Chabot was acting for Danton. One of the men Danton had sent to England, Talon, apparently tried to get a similar sum of money from Pitt, but without success.[6]

If Danton was really concerned to save the king's life and not merely to enrich himself, he went about it in an odd way. He concluded his speech of 30 November on the need for a sympathetic understanding of peasant unrest, with a gratuitous proposal that the king should be speedily tried, the very thing that he had

5. Quoted in C. Becker, 'A letter from Danton to Marie Antoinette', *American Historical Review*, 1921, p. 33.
6. A. Mathiez, *Danton et la paix,* Ch. 3.

told Lameth it was necessary to avoid. It is impossible to know whether or not he made any serious effort to save Louis XVI. There were many rumours that deputies were being bribed on the one side, as they were being intimidated on the other, and these could refer to the activities of an organisation with Danton at its head, but that would be mere conjecture. He himself was absent on mission in Belgium during most of the trial. He returned to Paris on 14 January and took no part in the voting on the following day, when Louis was declared guilty and the Convention rejected a motion to submit his sentence to a referendum. Once the issue was settled, Danton, as he had warned Lameth, made up for his previous silence by a display of enthusiasm. When the deputies voted on the king's fate, on 16 January, he said 'The only place to strike kings is on the head' and voted for the death penalty. On the same day he declared that a Spanish attempt to intercede for Louis merited an instant declaration of war. If Spanish Bourbons had been paying him, he proved a bad investment and Pitt could congratulate himself on his far-sighted parsimony.

To understand what Danton was doing in Belgium and to follow his relationship with Dumouriez, who commanded there, it is necessary to refer back to the events of the previous spring and summer. According to Danton, Dumouriez had offered him a ministerial post in March or April. The two had got on well together at the time of Valmy since both agreed that the Prussian army should be allowed to retreat unmolested. When Dumouriez had returned to a triumphant reception in Paris, as the hero of Valmy, Danton welcomed him in his capacity as president of the Jacobins and accompanied him to the opera. While Danton was Minister of Justice and working with Servan at the War Office, important contracts had been negotiated for supplying Dumouriez's army, notably with the abbé d'Espagnac. Talon and his uncle, Saint-Foy, were in the same business and when Saint-Foy was subsequently put on trial for fraud, Paré presided over the court that acquitted him.[7] One of Mirabeau's former secretaries claimed that Danton himself was involved in speculation with Dumouriez, Talon, Talleyrand (like Talon, sent on a mission to England), and Saint-Foy. All this suggests that there was a group of con-

7. A. Mathiez, *La corruption parlementaire sous la Terreur*, Ch. 5. *Autour de Danton*, Paris, 1926, Ch. 5; *Danton et la paix*, Ch. 3.

tractors of whom at least one (Talon) had a royalist past, approved by Dumouriez and protected by Danton and Servan. D'Espagnac's contract was ruinously expensive but Dumouriez maintained that it was necessary if his army was to be properly supplied.

This happy state of affairs was upset when Pache replaced Servan at the War Office in October and Cambon denounced the extravagance of Dumouriez and d'Espagnac on 22 November. The Convention ordered d'Espagnac's arrest, together with that of two army supply officers, Malus and Petitjean. Dumouriez sent them back to Paris with Westermann, now serving under him, as their spokesman. In the meantime the advent of Pache brought a drastic change at the War Office, whose bureaux were 'revolutionised'. Old bureaucrats were swept from their positions and replaced by political radicals, notably Vincent and Ronsin.[8] These two were Cordeliers and perhaps former members of Danton's machine, but they had their own way to make and Ronsin had been disappointed in his hopes of election to the Convention. They represented the new generation of Cordeliers and probably felt that they had been abandoned by their old leaders who had moved on to higher things. Pache resolved to do away with private war contracting, replacing the contractors with a state purchasing commission. If Dumouriez had any personal interest in d'Espagnac's contract he would be unlikely to appreciate this. He maintained, perhaps rightly, that the purchasing commission was inefficient and was jeopardising the future operations of his army. Ronsin, who replaced Malus and was also entrusted with the application of revolutionary legislation in 'liberated' Belgium, no doubt saw things rather differently.

What was happening was a new polarisation of revolutionary politics which extended well beyond the provisioning of Dumouriez's army, nothing less, in fact, than the emergence of the two factions that were eventually to tear the Montagnards to pieces. Behind Dumouriez were Danton, Fabre (involved in war-contracting on his own account), Westermann and presumably Delacroix, Danton's inseparable partner in Belgium, the nucleus of what was later to be regarded as a 'Dantonist' faction. Like the other groups, it was supported by a shoal of small fry such as Mergez (now serving with Dumouriez) and Noël, who

8. General Herlaut, *Le général rouge Ronsin*, Paris, 1956, *passim*.

97

was based in England but visited both Danton and Dumouriez in Belgium. Dumouriez, understandably full of his own importance as the man who had turned back the Prussians and driven the Austrians out of Belgium, was impatient of what he regarded as the bungling of an incompetent revolutionary government, at the mercy of an ignorant and fanatical Convention. He was inclined to treat Belgium as his private fief, complained that the purchasing commission was wrecking his army and repeatedly offered his resignation. Pache insisted that all was well. Uncertain what to make of the conflicting evidence, the Convention, at the end of November, decided to send four of its members to Belgium to investigate. Danton and Delacroix were two of them, presumably by their own choice. Danton was probably regarded, and regarded himself, as the best man to talk to Dumouriez. If he was also looking for a pretext to be away from Paris during the king's trial, he returned a few days too soon.

While he and Delacroix were back in Paris, between the 14th and 31st of January, a political offensive was mounted against the War Office. On the 21st Danton told the Convention that the army in Belgium was being starved of provisions and equipment. While disclaiming any intention of making a personal attack on Pache, he said that the War Office was too heavy a burden for one man and hinted that someone else should be put in charge of the logistical side of things. On the day he returned to Belgium, Desfieux, a member of the correspondence committee of the Jacobins who was to make himself very conspicuous in the coming months, attacked Pache in the club. Four days later Pache was replaced by Beurnonville, a general who had fought under Dumouriez at Valmy and Jemappes. This was promptly followed by the dismissal of Vincent and the sansculottes from the War Office. In the meantime Delacroix and Camus (two of the four deputies sent to Belgium) persuaded the Convention to wind up the purchasing commission. Malus and Petitjean were sent back to Belgium and Ronsin was recalled. The Assembly renewed its committee on war contracts, making Julien de Toulouse, a friend of d'Espagnac, the chairman of the new committee. On 17 February Julien reported on behalf of the committee that d'Espagnac had more than fulfilled his contract, on terms advantageous to the Republic. On the motion of Thuriot, a friend of Danton's, d'Espagnac was then released.

Dumouriez's enemies had been routed all along the line.

When Danton returned from his second visit to Belgium, on 16 February, he found tragedy waiting for him at home, where his wife had died during his absence. He is said to have been so overwhelmed with grief that he had her body exhumed so that he could take a last farewell, a story that gains credibility from the fact that the sculptor, Deseine, exhibited at the salon of 1793 a bust of Gabrielle, 'exhumed after seven days'. Robespierre sent Danton the most moving letter he ever wrote to anyone, claiming to be his 'tender and devoted friend . . . I love you more than ever, to the death. At this moment I am your second self.' We know so little about Danton as a private individual that there is no means of telling what Gabrielle's death meant to him. The fact that he re-married within a few months need not imply a lack of feeling. He had a young family to look after and Gabrielle is said to have urged Louise Gély, a friend of the family and barely fifteen, to take care of her two boys. Louise is believed to have insisted, not merely on a religious marriage but on one celebrated by a priest who had refused to accept the revolutionary religious settlement, and Danton to have complied. His home meant a great deal to him, whether it was the flat in Paris or the house he had bought in Arcis. He was a family man as well as a revolutionary, unlike a good many of his colleagues; but the Revolution imposed its own harsh discipline and a fortnight after his tragic homecoming he was on the road to Belgium once again.

VII Danton, Dumouriez and the Girondins

When Danton got back to Brussels on 5 March 1793 there was plenty to take his mind off his private grief. Dumouriez had invaded Holland in February and was going well. On 1 March the Austrians replied with an offensive into Belgium, designed to take him in the rear and threaten his communications. This went well too, threw back the French armies and threatened Liège. As the French right flank began to collapse, Dumouriez, confident that he could soon force the Dutch to make peace, insisted on continuing his own offensive, until the Convention ordered him back into Belgium, on 8 March. Danton and Delacroix hastily organised the evacuation of Church valuables from Liège. As usual in time of military defeat, there were plenty of opportunities for individual enterprise. Everything was justified that kept treasure out of enemy hands and much of it ended up in hands that were friendly enough, but not those intended by the authorities. The commune of Béthune arrested two wagons, loaded with cases addressed to Danton and Delacroix, on the ground that the carter's papers were not in order. The two deputies subsequently claimed that they had placed their own scanty effects in carts full of public property, which had given rise to an unfortunate misunderstanding. This does not sound very likely. At the time of Danton's trial the Montagnard deputy, Levasseur, said that Danton had used his political influence to keep the report from Béthune out of the way of the Committee of Public Safety. Madame Le Bas, the widow of a former member of the Committee of General Security, told the historian, Buchez, that her husband had proof of the theft by Danton and Delacroix, but that this was suppressed by Courtois when he edited Robespierre's papers. This presumably refers to the same incident and it sounds probable enough, but Danton was not the man to worry about probabilities and, as usual, nothing was made public at the time and the evidence that has survived falls just short of proof.[1]

1. This evidence is summarised in A. Mathiez, *Autour de Danton*, Paris, 1926, Ch. 8.

Danton was back in Paris to report, from 8 March to 17 March, just in time for the mysterious abortive insurrection of the 9th–10th, in which he was later accused of being involved. The military situation, so favourable at the end of 1792, had deteriorated with bewildering speed, for a major civil war had broken out in the west about the time that the Belgian front had given way. Everyone's thoughts turned to the parallel with the previous summer, when invasion had brought the prison massacres. On 8 March Delacroix informed the Convention of the evacuation of Liège and Aix-la-Chapelle and demanded the suspension of army leave and the immediate return of all troops to the front. Supporting him, Robespierre, who was usually something of an alarmist, took a reassuring line and insisted that the reverses in Belgium were only temporary. This was not enough for Danton who raised the spectre of the encirclement of Dumouriez and the 'death of 60,000 Frenchmen'. He demanded the immediate reinforcement of Dumouriez – which could only be done by raising volunteers in Paris, as in the previous September, and persuaded the Convention to send deputies to the Sections that night to appeal for men. Warning his colleagues against their tendency to make a scapegoat of every unsuccessful general, he praised the ability of Dumouriez. 'History will judge his talent, his passions and his vices; what is certain is that his interests are bound up with the glory of the Republic.' Despite the gravity of the crisis, the Assembly was not to be diverted from a long wrangle about the Girondin and Montagnard press. When the next session opened equally inauspiciously with an argument about whether to discuss the military situation or disorder in Paris, Danton intervened with the unexpected proposal to abolish imprisonment for debt: 'Respect poverty and the poor will respect the rich'. This looked like an indication that he feared another attack on the prisons and hoped to save at least one category of unfortunates. His motion was voted and the deputies then went back to their recriminations about the press.

Danton had reason to think that the situation in Paris was getting out of control. At the Jacobins on the evening of 8 March there had been demands for the creation of a revolutionary tribunal and its use against the Girondins. Desfieux proposed the arrest of all those denounced and Hébert demanded the execution of all generals and ministers. On the following night Desfieux suggested forcing the Convention to purge its committees and arrest the ministers. Addressing a public meeting outside the club, he urged it to demand the punishment of all conspirators. While this was going on, several hundred men were roaming the streets and smashing some of the Girondin printing presses. On 10 March the Assembly was apprehensive about its own safety. Danton, as he had done on 2 September, tried to divert the agitation towards national defence. He praised Dumouriez and held out the hope that victory in Holland might precipitate revolution in England.

> Look, citizens, at the fine future ahead of you. You have an entire nation for lever, liberty and reason as your fulcrum and you still haven't overturned the world! . . . I was in just such a position when the enemy had penetrated into France [in September]. I told them, the false patriots, 'Your quarrels are harming the triumph of liberty. I reject the lot of you; you are all traitors. Let's defeat the enemy and then argue.' I said, 'What do I care if my name is dishonoured?' I agreed to pass as a *buveur de sang*! Let us drink the blood of the enemies of humanity if we have to, but let Europe be free!

Turning against those who accused the Convention of ruining the rich, he warned them to take care. 'Let the rich listen! If our conquests don't pay our debts, the rich will have to pay them themselves – and soon.' His peroration sounds like a conscious evocation of his great speech of 2 September:

> We need a great effort, one great blow. Seize Holland, rally the *patriotes* in England, let France march and the nation is saved! You will go down to posterity in glory. Accomplish your destiny. No more passion, no more quarrels, on with the crest of the wave of liberty!

In the evening session he said much of it again and secured a vote for the immediate creation of a revolutionary tribunal, on the ground that the existence of a similar court would have averted the September massacres. 'Let *us* be terrible, to dispense the people from the need to be terrible themselves.' His conclusion echoed what he had said earlier in the day:

> To sum up, tonight: organization of the tribunal, organization

of the executive; tomorrow: military activity – send out your commissioners, let the whole of France rise, take up arms and march on the enemy; invade Holland, free Belgium, destroy the trade of England – may the friends of liberty triumph there – and our arms, everywhere victorious, carry happiness and liberation to the peoples of the world!

No one else could have said it and it brought the deputies to their feet. It was a pity the Girondins missed it, but most of them had stayed away in case they were attacked in the Convention itself. They had reason to be apprehensive.[2] Desfieux demanded their arrest, at the Jacobins – he seemed determined to have *someone* arrested. There was talk of murdering them and the Cordeliers actually called for an insurrection and tried to raise the Sections. The Jacobins and the Commune refused to budge and Santerre, the Commander-in-Chief of the National Guard, dominated the streets with his patrols. The whole business is very obscure and the would-be insurrectionaries were little-known men: Fournier, Varlet, perhaps Proli and Pereira, with Desfieux as a fellow-traveller. When it was all over no one knew quite what to make of it and, as usual, everyone suspected some kind of a plot. The Commune thought – or at least said – that royalists had tried to exploit the agitation for their own ends. One argument later advanced was that the object of the agitation was to provide Dumouriez with a pretext for marching on Paris to suppress anarchy, and that Danton was a party to the plot. So far as Danton himself is concerned, it surely defies credibility that the author of the passionate patriotic speeches in the Convention was laying his bets in exactly the opposite direction. The evidence for the intrigue itself, which many historians have taken seriously, is very sketchy. The only would-be insurgents who are known to have had any previous contact with Dumouriez are Desfieux and Proli, whose rôles on 10 March seem to have been somewhat marginal. A more serious objection to the 'Dumouriez plot' is that there is no evidence that Dumouriez was plotting – yet. In the days of his victories he had been quite happy about the overthrow of the monarchy and had written cheerfully to a fellow-general in October 1792: 'That's how we do things in a republic; it

2. A. M. Boursier, 'L'émeute parisienne du 10 mars 1793', in *Annales historiques de la Révolution française,* 1972.

would never have been possible with a king.' Since then his quarrel with the War Office had no doubt altered his views about how things were done in a republic, but he was still hoping to carve out some sort of a position for himself by the conquest of Holland. It was not until he returned to Brussels on 10 March – the day of the disorder in Paris – and discovered how the goodwill of 'his' Belgians had been dissipated by French plundering and the intemperate application of revolutionary legislation by men like Ronsin, that he finally exploded. He wrote a scorching letter to the Convention on 12 March, denouncing Pache's conduct at the War Office and Cambon's policy of plunder and informing the Assembly that, on his own authority, he had provisionally suspended all orders for the 'revolutionising' of Belgium. It was not until his defeat at Neerwinden on the 18th had put paid to his military ambitions that he seems to have contemplated marching on Paris.

If there was no 'Dumouriez plot' on 10 March, the most sensible explanation of Danton's behaviour is the obvious one. Obsessed by memories of both the shame and the glory of September, he tried to avert the former and revive the latter by a combination of an active military policy and an effective repressive one. Like Robespierre and some of the more responsible Girondins, his main preoccupation was national defence and it was not his fault if others were more concerned with scoring party points. His biographer, Hérissay, claims that there was a last attempt at reconciliation between Danton and the Girondins, about 15 March, when one of them replied to Danton's overtures, 'No amnesty for the September murderers. War! And may one side perish!'[3] If this is true, it makes Danton's involvement in the insurrectionary agitation even more unlikely.

The receipt of Dumouriez's letter on 15 March stretched to the limit the tenuous link between the general and the Assembly. The latter's president kept the letter secret and passed it on to the Committee of General Defence. One of the members of the committee, Barère – not a particularly reliable witness – wrote in his memoirs that he proposed the arrest of Dumouriez. Danton and Delacroix opposed this and offered to make yet another visit to Belgium and either induce the Commander-in-Chief to with-

3. J. Hérissay, *Cet excellent M. Danton*, Paris, 1960, pp. 278–9.

draw his letter or return and denounce him to the Convention. There was probably nothing sinister about Danton's continuing support for Dumouriez. He paid little attention to any rhetoric, including his own, and was always confident of his ability to make opponents recognise what seemed to him common sense. All the deputies who had been in Belgium were agreed that Dumouriez was popular with his troops. Danton argued that to dismiss him would disorganise and demoralise the army, and to arrest him was something easier to vote in Paris than to execute at his own headquarters. The Committee of General Defence, presumably converted by Danton, agreed to make a last attempt to get Dumouriez to retract his letter.

Danton and Delacroix therefore set out on their final mission to Belgium on 17 or 18 March. When Danton met Dumouriez on the night of the 20–21st the general had been defeated at Neerwinden. He could no longer think of dictating terms to the Assembly from a position of strength; he was incensed by the creation of the revolutionary tribunal and had no intention of becoming one of its victims. By the time he saw Danton he was probably contemplating some sort of intervention in Paris, although he did not contact the Austrians with a view to arranging an armistice until the 23rd. According to Danton, Dumouriez showed him a letter from Roland, inviting him to join forces with the Girondins and destroy the Montagnards in general and Danton in particular. Roland denied this and it sounds unlikely. The most that Danton could extract from Dumouriez was a curt letter to the Convention, asking it to suspend judgement on his previous letter of the 12th.

Having failed to get any satisfaction out of Dumouriez, Danton left him, returned to Paris . . . and disappeared. Unless he lingered in Belgium for reasons that he never divulged, he must have been back in Paris by 23 March, but he did not inform the Committee of General Defence of the failure of his mission until the 26th. As usual, he had a defence that was more of a smokescreen than an explanation: he had reached Paris, exhausted, between eight and nine at night and was not even aware that the committee was in session. It seems to have taken him rather a long time to find out. In a speech on 1 April he is reported to have said that he did not return to Paris until the 29th. If this was correctly reported, he must have forgotten that he had spoken in the Convention on the 27th. Where he actually was and what he was doing will probably never be known.

In the meantime, after he had already come to terms with the Austrians, Dumouriez had several meetings with three Jacobins, Proly, Dubuisson and Pereira, who had apparently gone to see him on their own initiative. According to their account, he told them that he intended to destroy the Convention and restore the constitution of 1791, which involved restoring some kind of monarchy. He invited them to launch an insurrection in Paris while he marched on the capital. They pretended to agree, in order to escape, and once away from his headquarters, denounced him to the deputies on mission in Belgium and to the Convention. If Dumouriez did reveal his plans to the Jacobin trio, he presumably told Danton as well. Dumouriez, in his memoirs, said that only four people knew of his intention to restore the 1791 constitution. His editor, without revealing his sources, said that three of these were Danton, Delacroix and Westermann – which can only be true if he counted Proly, Dubuisson and Pereira as one.

One can only speculate about where Danton actually stood. It would have been in character for him to defer making any choice for as long as possible and to insure himself with both sides. He may well have thought that there was something to be said for a constitutional monarchy with Chartres – who was serving with Dumouriez – as king. The most likely explanation of his conduct is that he decided to wait and see what happened before joining the side that looked most likely to win. When he did go to the Committee of General Defence, on 26 March, he persuaded his colleagues to take no action until Dumouriez had extricated his army from Belgium. This could have been military prudence, but it was politically ambiguous. Robespierre, who had previously been in favour of giving Dumouriez the benefit of the doubt, was by now proposing his arrest.

It is unlikely that Danton gave Dumouriez the benefit of anything more than his neutrality. On 27 March he urged the Convention to forget its quarrels – in which context his 'revelation' that Roland had sought the general's support against the Montagnards was scarcely helpful – and direct popular enthusiasm towards national defence and the suppression of counter-revolutionary activities. He persuaded his colleagues to vote for the immediate creation of the revolutionary tribunal, which can hardly have endeared him to Dumouriez. What he did *not* do was give any public account of what he had discovered in Belgium. When Proli and his two colleagues informed the Committee of General Defence of Dumouriez's treason, Danton found himself in an awkward situation. On the 29th Marat demanded that he make a report, but the Girondin, Lasource, rather ominously persuaded the Assembly to wait until Danton and Dumouriez could be confronted with each other. On the following day, when Danton joined in Montagnard criticism of the Girondins, he was taunted for his silence about what was happening in Belgium and his failure to account for the money he spent when minister was raked up against him once again. Marat renewed his demand for an explanation at the Jacobins on the 31st and wanted to know why Danton had said nothing to the Assembly. If Danton had been playing a waiting game, he seems to have realised that it could go on no longer. He denounced Dumouriez and promised to explain himself to the Convention on the following day. He gave the club a preview of his future tactics by a diversion in which he invited the Jacobins to organise a campaign of public pressure on the Convention to expel those of its members who had refused to vote for the king's death. In private, he was to complain that it was the Girondins who thwarted his attempts to keep the republicans united, but it looks as though his own devious tactics and determination to back every horse in the race got him into a predicament where he could only conciliate the Montagnards by himself resorting to baiting their opponents.

The important debate on 1 April opened badly for Danton with the reading of a letter from Proli, Dubuisson and Pereira that revealed the extent of Dumouriez's disaffection and naturally raised the awkward question of Danton's silence. He was blamed, not merely for his failure to report to the Assembly but also for persuading the Committee of General Defence to keep Dumouriez's original letter secret. In reply, Danton tried to win the sympathy of the deputies by claiming that he and Delacroix had been under fire at Neerwinden, which was untrue. He then embarked on an ingenious defence of his policy with regard to Dumouriez, subdued in tone, that carefully concealed his silence between 23 and 26 March. He was never very good on the defensive and he exposed himself to a stinging reply from the irreconcilable Girondin, Lasource. In a speech that combined legitimate criticism with distortion and innuendo, Lasource implied that Danton and Delacroix were accomplices of Dumouriez and demanded an investigation of their conduct. Birotteau chimed in with the accusation – promptly denied – that Fabre d'Eglantine had hinted to the Committee of General Defence that the monarchy should be restored. Danton remained virtually silent while the Convention voted to set up a commission to investigate the behaviour of its representatives in Belgium. When he demanded an explanation from Cambon about money that he and Delacroix had received for their mission, there were shouts that this should be referred to the commission. When Danton went submissively back to his place it looked as though he was defeated. His Montagnard colleagues and the crowd in the public galleries clamoured for him to clear himself and with their encouragement he returned to the rostrum in a very different mood.

There followed an extraordinary scene in which Danton, with Marat acting as his prompter, turned on the Girondins. He began by apologising to the Montagnards for disregarding their advice that any compromise with the Girondins was out of the question. He denounced those who had tried to save the king, the tactic he had tried out the previous night at the Jacobins. His reply to Lasource was more vehement than convincing, especially when he claimed that he had not returned to Paris until the 29th, but the Montagnards would not look too critically at anyone who attacked their opponents. Gradually he worked himself into a passion that was realistic if not, perhaps, quite real:

DANTON: Do you want to know who I mean?
          (Shouts of 'Yes! Yes!')
DANTON: Listen!
MARAT: Listen!
DANTON: Do you want the whole thing in one word?
          (Shouts of 'Yes! Yes!')
DANTON: I believe no truce is possible between the Mountain,
          between the *patriotes* who wanted the king's death
          and the cowards who slandered us throughout
          France in the hope of saving him!
          *(Many of the Left rise to their feet and applaud.
          Shouts of 'We shall save the country!')*

There was a good deal more of the same thing. Danton repeated his disculpation two or three times, combining it with abuse of the Girondins, notably of Roland, and demanded that the commission that was to be set up should investigate the conduct of every deputy since the Convention first met, a demand that was as difficult to reject as it would have been impossible to implement. At last he returned to his seat, acclaimed and embraced by the Montagnards, and that was the last that was heard of any investigation of his relations with Dumouriez.

It was a *tour de force,* a brilliant combination of passion and calculation. His attack on those who had refused to vote for the king's death was a shrewd political blow. Many of the Girondins were in fact regicides but they would have no option but to defend those of their supporters who were not, and thereby tar the whole group with the royalist brush. Danton had saved himself and recovered the enthusiastic support of the Montagnards, but he paid a high price for his equivocation over Dumouriez. Self-preservation bound him to the Montagnards and deprived him of his freedom of manoeuvre. Despite his repudiation of the Girondins on 1 April he was subsequently to make overtures to them, in the Assembly, but he took care to insure himself by denouncing them in the Jacobins. They were naturally inclined to suspect him of hypocrisy and they may have been right. Perhaps he had never had much to lose, for ever since the Convention met the Girondins had preferred to exploit his dubious reputation against his fellow-Montagnards rather than to take advantage of his offers of cooperation. It was, after all, Lasource who had provoked him into a declaration of war. But Danton was a moderate by temperament, as well as a man who disliked making enemies, and this was a choice that he probably regretted.

There was another respect in which the sequel to the Dumouriez affair weakened his position. The Convention had sent Beurnonville, the Minister of War, with four deputies to arrest Dumouriez, who handed them all over to the Austrians. Beurnonville was then replaced by Bouchotte, who brought back into the War Office Vincent, Ronsin and all their sansculotte following. Danton, who had been singing the praises of Paris, the Sections and the 'people' all through the military crisis, had nothing to fear from this, but his side had lost the battle for the War Office. The arrest of the war contractor, d'Espagnac, as an accomplice of Dumouriez, was ordered on the same day that Danton scored his oratorical triumph. D'Espagnac went into hiding and wrote to Julien de Toulouse, imploring his protection and even offering to make him his heir. Westermann, too, was arrested and accused of manoeuvring his troops to threaten Lille at a time when Dumouriez was trying to seize Valenciennes, Condé and Lille to cover his march on Paris.[4] Westermann was to be acquitted in May but the stigma would remain. Danton himself may not have been closely associated with d'Espagnac or known what Westermann was doing, but they were his kind of people and their misfortune augured him no good.

When Dumouriez's army refused to support him he fled to the Austrians, followed soon afterwards by Chartres. This averted any immediate danger to Paris, which was still defended by a French army, if a defeated and disorganised one. The allied forces advanced slowly into France, besieging the frontier forts on their way. This respite allowed the Convention to devote most of its time to the dangerous delights of party politics. The Girondins accused their opponents of trying to whip up feelings in Paris for a forcible purge of the Assembly. No doubt some Montagnards would have welcomed this and Danton himself had seemed to advocate it in his speech to the Jacobins on 31 March. The majority, however, either because they feared that an insurrection would fail or because they were apprehensive about unleashing a popular movement that they might not be able to control, stuck to constitutional methods. The Montagnards tried to discredit their opponents by presenting them as partisans of Dumouriez and Orleans. These were not plausible charges and the presence of Danton on the Montagnard benches must have been something of a liability. Weeks went by in inconclusive wrangling. The March crisis had at least convinced most of the deputies of the need for a more effective executive. The large and unwieldy Committee of General Defence, whose meetings were attended by any deputies who chose, was replaced by a Committee of Public Safety, originally limited to nine members and meeting in secret. The new committee, which was eventually to develop into a war cabinet, began modestly enough but it was obviously likely to become a body of some importance. When its members were chosen, on 7 April, the fact that Danton won the fifth place suggested that he had recovered the confidence of the Assembly. Delacroix

4. Archives Nationales, F⁷ 4775⁵¹

was elected with him and so was Cambon, all the members being drawn from the more moderate of the Montagnards.[5]

During the two months that separated the Dumouriez crisis from the overthrow of the Girondins on 2 June, Danton's policy was as ambiguous as usual. In the Assembly he appealed for unity. Only three days after his declaration of war on the Girondins, on 4 April, he appealed to both sides: 'Let us draw together fraternally; the safety of all of us is at stake. If the [Dumouriez] conspiracy triumphs it will mean the proscription of all those who have ever been known as *patriotes,* without making any distinction between shades of opinion.' A fortnight later he agreed with the Girondin orator, Vergniaud, that there was no need to specify freedom of religious opinion in the new constitution, since this was a matter of course, and he drew the appropriate moral: 'When it is a question concerning human happiness we are all agreed'. This may well have been what Danton would have liked, but the Girondins must have suspected that his real intention was merely to disarm their suspicions. On 2 April he suggested to the Jacobins bringing back the deputies – mostly Montagnards – who had been sent into the provinces to supervise the raising of conscripts, in order 'to purge the Convention of all the cowardly intriguers'. Perhaps he was still smarting from Lasource's attack on the previous day. He certainly did nothing positive to support those who were talking of a forcible purge. What he did do, repeatedly, was to insist that the Assembly was in no danger and should not attach any importance to such evidence of insurrectionary plotting as came to light. On 10 April he and Fabre tried to prevent the reading of a petition for the prosecution of the leading Girondins, from the Halle au Blé Section, lest this should give rise to demands for punitive action against the Section. On 1 May he persuaded his colleagues to disregard an unflattering declaration by the faubourg Saint-Antoine to the effect that the Assembly had done nothing for the country. Towards the middle of the month he opposed the arrest of Chaumette, the *procureur* of the Paris Commune, on a charge of delivering arms to would-be insurgents. Such moves were second nature to Danton. They were both demonstrations of loyalty to the Montagnards and reassurances to the timid that they had nothing to fear. If nothing happened, Danton would be

5. For Danton's activities on the Committee of Public Safety, see Chapter 8.

vindicated by the non-event and if anything did happen he would probably be on the winning side himself and if not could always plead that he had been right most of the time and only wrong once. Whether – or when – he himself came to believe that an insurrection was necessary is a question that he would probably have regarded as academic in both senses of the word. If a revolt succeeded, he had been hinting at its necessity for months; if none happened, he had always said that there was no danger; if it failed, he had had nothing to do with it.

The one positive note that he struck was his insistence on doing something about the social problems of the sansculottes. This had been a constant theme since March, when he began appealing in general terms for the support of the poor against the rich. On 4 April – that first week of April was certainly a busy time for him – he persuaded the Assembly to vote for the creation of a paid sansculotte militia and the imposition of special taxes on the rich in order to subsidise bread prices. A month later he renewed his demand for a paid militia, since nothing had been done to implement the earlier decision, and for the payment of the poorer citizens who took time off work to attend meetings of the Sections. The Convention applauded him but did nothing. The militia and the payment for attendance at the meetings of the Sections were to come in September. The former is generally regarded as a triumph for the 'popular movement' and for radicalism, which, in a sense, it was, but the motion had originally been made by Danton in the spring. The fact that he should have provided the extremists with their organisation, in the Cordelier club, their tactics and much of their programme is a warning against seeing the politics of the French Revolution in terms of ideology or class conflict. Politicians in search of a following could always hope to find one among the sansculottes. The means of attracting support and the ways of using it remained pretty much the same throughout the Revolution. They were taken up by one group after another and they could be exploited by Left or Right. Danton, a politician to his finger-tips, at least deserves the credit for having discovered them.

Towards the end of May the long-drawn-out struggle began to approach a climax. For some months there had been intermittent meetings of delegates from the Sections at the archbishop's palace, to discuss violent action against the Assembly. These had been countenanced by Pache, who was now mayor of Paris, but they do not appear to have been under his control. The Jacobins viewed them with some suspicion since the delegates were inclined to advocate murdering unpopular deputies and it was suspected that the meetings had been infiltrated by royalist agents, only too happy at the prospect of getting the revolutionaries to destroy each other. The Convention, alarmed by reports of these gatherings, voted on 18 May to create a commission of twelve deputies to investigate the alleged threats of an insurrection. There were no Montagnards on this commission and the Montagnard deputy, Levasseur, believed that some of its members were more royalist than Girondin. The Twelve set to work with some vigour. On 24 May they proposed reinforcing the National Guard patrols round the Convention, obliging all citizens to perform their guard service, closing the Sections at 10 p.m. to prevent a militant rump from passing radical resolutions after the majority had gone home, and preventing men from one Section attending meetings of another, a tactic used by the radicals to pack meetings. Danton opposed these measures with some ingenuity. By pretending that the threat of insurrection came from the Right, he was able to denounce all 'aristocrats' and insist that the existing laws gave the deputies adequate protection against counter-revolutionaries. He could just possibly have believed this to be the case, for two of the men arrested for urging the meeting at the archbishop's palace to murder some of the deputies were police officers who were later to be executed as royalist agents.

When the commission extended its operations and arrested Hébert, of the Commune, and Dobsen, the president of the Section where the insurrectionary meetings were held, the Montagnards found themselves between two fires. They were not in control of the movement at the archbishop's palace, which they may have suspected, and they were now threatened by effective repressive action by the Twelve, which looked like undermining their position in Paris, where the Girondins had more support than is generally recognised. Some of the Montagnard leaders apparently concluded that they would have to act before it was too late. They planned a 'moral insurrection', the application of controlled pressure to induce the Convention itself to expel the most important Girondins. A speech by Danton on 28 May hinted at this change of tactics, when he threatened an insurrection if Hébert and Dobsen were not released. Later in the day he returned to the charge: 'The time has come for the people to renounce defensive tactics and attack all the agents of *modérantisme*'. Robespierre took much the same line at the Jacobins on the following night. Everything was couched in the conditional tense and in abstract terms, but it was probably a sign that the Montagnards had resigned themselves to action. Cambon was to tell the Convention in 1795 that he was one of six members of the Committee of Public Safety to sign a secret denunciation of Robespierre and Danton, who were said to be holding secret meetings at Charenton, with Pache and members of the Commune. According to Cambon, when Danton was accused by his colleagues on the committee of aspiring to a position of domination, he replied, 'It's true we have dined together, but you have nothing to fear. We are going to save liberty.'

On 31 May the tocsin rang to signal a day of confused petitioning and demonstrating. The men from the archbishop's palace overthrew the Commune but then reinstated its members. They seem to have allowed themselves to be merged with the 'moral insurrection' group, which effectively neutralised them. Garat, who had replaced Roland at the Interior earlier in the year, met Danton outside the Convention at dawn and Danton said to him, 'It will be nothing; we must let them smash a few presses'. This was presumably intended to deter Garat from taking any repressive action, for when a deputation from the Commune reached the Assembly, Danton is said to have presented it with the text of a petition for the arrest of twenty-two Girondin leaders. This was all in accordance with Montagnard tactics, but the 'moral insurrection' was too moral and not insurrectionary enough to frighten the majority of the deputies into voting for a purge. Danton tried to deter the Assembly from taking effective action against the insurrection and to persuade the moderates to accept the purge. He foiled those who wanted to interrogate Hanriot, who had been put in command of the National Guard by the insurgents, on the capital charge of failing to prevent the firing of the alarm gun. With more impudence than plausibility, he maintained that the firing of the gun was merely a signal for the good people of Paris to bring their problems to the Assembly. 'If some really dangerous men, from whatever party, should want to prolong the agitation after it has served its purpose, Paris itself will annihilate them, once you have seen to it that justice is done.' This Sybilline advice was presumably a hint to the Centre that if it wanted a quiet life, all it had to do was to vote for the arrest of the Girondins. Perhaps there was a hint too that 'really danger- ous men' were indeed at large, but that the Montagnards had brought them under control.

Unconvinced and insufficiently intimidated, the Assembly con- tented itself with voting the abolition of the Twelve and referred the demand for a purge to the Committee of Public Safety, which was a polite way of burying it. When 1 June proved equally in- conclusive it looked as though the 'insurrection' was running out of steam. By the 2nd, however, the Commune was sufficiently confident of its authority to subject the Assembly to the kind of pressure it had itself denounced only two days earlier. Hanriot blockaded the Convention with a ring of National Guards. The deputies, in solemn procession, tried to break through but were repulsed. Back in their seats, they reluctantly voted to put the leading Girondins under house arrest. A small core of Montagnards such as Robespierre welcomed this intervention of the 'sovereign people', but many of their own group, together with the great majority of the uncommitted deputies, resented the humiliation of the Assembly. Danton does not seem to have committed himself either way. There is a story that he was invited to use his influence to bring the insurrection to an end but replied that he could not trust the Girondins, which was reasonable enough since their first reaction, if they had won, would have been to turn against him. A year later Saint-Just accused him of calling for Hanriot's head and then laughing the matter off when he got no support. Danton had opposed Pache over the business of war contracting and Pache was now mayor of Paris. Men from the War Office were said by Cambon to have taken a leading part in the insurrec- tion and they were no friends of his. When the movement had succeeded he naturally claimed to have supported it from the start. So did everyone else. Danton would probably have preferred, if he could, to have obtained the same result by petitioning and a free vote of the deputies. This had proved impracticable and he could scarcely regret the disappearance of the men who had been taunting him for the past six months, especially since they had merely been arrested and it did not look as though they would come to any harm. On the other hand, he was losing his freedom of manoeuvre all the time. The royalist option had gone when Chartres followed Dumouriez to the Austrians; with the purge of the Girondins, the majority of the deputies, whatever their private views, would not risk another insurrection by challenging the Montagnards. Danton's future would have to lie with the Mountain, but there seemed no reason why it should not be comfortable enough. He was popular with the Jacobins, the obvious man to conciliate the Centre, which held the majority in the Assembly, and the leading member of the Committee of Public Safety. All the Montagnards were concerned to win acceptance by the country as a whole of what their opponents denounced as a Parisian coup d'état, and Danton was the man to make moderation sound exciting. If he looked back to the difficult days at the end of March, Danton must have felt that things had turned out rather well.

VIII The Elder Statesman

Throughout the summer of 1793 the immediate question was whether the country as a whole would accept the Parisian coup d'état. A considerable area in the west remained under royalist control. The great commercial cities of Lyons and Marseilles were in the hands of men who repudiated the Montagnards as puppets of the Parisian mob and they were soon joined by Bordeaux. Most of the local authorities at first refused to recognise the legitimacy of the purged Assembly and the more resolute announced their intention of raising men for a march on the capital. Bearing in mind the fact that France was also at war with Austria, Prussia, Great Britain, Spain and Holland, the Montagnards had no alternative but to preach conciliation at home, some on principle and others from expediency. The more moderate gave the impression that they deplored the forcible methods used by the Commune on 2 June and the Commune itself vehemently condemned any talk of further violence. The Parisian Sections were divided, two of them even sending representatives to negotiate with rebels in Normandy who had raised a makeshift army that tried to advance up the Seine to Paris. Within the capital itself radicalism was for the moment confined to a handful of men, known as the Enragés, who demanded more state intervention on behalf of the poor, the expulsion of nobles from the army and the violent repression of all forms of counter-revolution. For a time the Enragé leader, Jacques Roux, managed to win over the Cordeliers, but the established politicians of every persuasion saw his movement as a challenge to their own authority or ambition and Roux had little chance of making much headway in the face of the Jacobins and the Commune. This was a period of uncertain Montagnard leadership with no clear lines of party division. Personal friends opposed each other's policies and men who were to become allies were confused with their future opponents in a kind of political vacuum.

The Committee of Public Safety that had been created in April had a chance to implement its own policies without any systematic opposition. The committee was originally intended to supervise the Council of Ministers. During the summer of 1793 it gradually extended the range of its powers until it became something like a war cabinet. Danton, who had taken charge of foreign policy, realised that to consolidate the revolution and avoid further violence it was necessary to disarm as many as possible of the Republic's embarrassing swarm of domestic and foreign enemies. To begin with, he tried to prolong Dumouriez's truce with the Austrians. Suspecting further treason, Robespierre on 13 April invited the Convention to vote the death penalty against anyone who should propose negotiating with the enemy. Danton objected that this would condemn the Republic to indefinite war. He went on to condemn the offer of fraternal help, extended in the optimistic days at the end of 1792 to any popular liberation movements abroad, on the sensible ground that it committed France to give military support to any handful of revolutionaries who might choose to take up arms against the Emperor of China. The Convention voted his motion to declare that it would not meddle in the internal affairs of other powers, but would bury itself under its own ruins rather than allow them to interfere in the politics of the Republic. It was his usual tactic, sweetening moderate policies by dressing them up in violent language. Robespierre's inconvenient motion was diluted to a vague and innocuous vote of death for anyone making an agreement with powers who did not recognise the independence and sovereignty of the French nation and the indivisibility of the Republic founded on liberty and equality. This gave Danton the free hand that he wanted.

Four days after the insurrection of 2 June his colleague, Barère, with Danton's support, made a singularly conciliatory policy statement to the Assembly in which he criticised the inquisitorial behaviour of the revolutionary committees of the Sections, demanded a proper election for the commander-in-chief of the National Guard – the post that Hanriot had held irregularly since 31 May – denounced any interference with the freedom of the mails and even offered to send deputies as hostages to the restive Departments. This was sailing too close to the wind and looked so much like a repudiation of the recent insurrection that it provoked a good many Montagnard objections. Danton came to Barère's rescue and had everything referred back to the Committee of Public Safety.

Not much is known about his attempts to deal with the protest movements in the provinces but it seems clear that he tried to buy them off. Deforgues, his former clerk who was soon to be made Foreign Minister, was sent into Normandy with this intention. The rebellious Committee of Public Safety that had been created at Montpellier in the south claimed to have a letter from Danton offering his protection on condition that they sent against the royalists in the Vendée the men they had originally raised for a march on Paris. Cambon, admittedly, was to claim in 1795 that Danton and Delacroix had thwarted the conciliatory views of the majority of their colleagues, but this was probably an attempt to justify himself at the expense of people who were no longer there to object; *de mortuis nil nisi malum* was established revolutionary doctrine. Granted Danton's indifference to his own reputation and to ideological posturing, together with his innocent faith in the power of money to heal all ills, it is very likely that he made the kind of offers that might take on a sinister appearance if quoted out of context at a time when revolutionary attitudes had hardened. He may have been responsible for the decision to send to the Vendée General Biron, a former duke and a suitable man to negotiate with the rebel gentry. Biron himself implied that his mission was diplomatic as well as military.

More important were Danton's attempts to break up the coalition of France's foreign enemies.[1] Everything about his contacts with England is obscure, from the time in 1789 when the French ambassador in London had believed him to be a British agent. Paine called himself 'your friend' and Noël claimed that Danton was in touch with a friend of Horne Tooke's. Acquaintances of this kind would hardly commend him to Pitt and in any case the British Government, while perhaps pretending to talk, could not be expected to call off a war that had hardly begun or to negotiate seriously with a committee which was only too likely to be repudiated by an Assembly that was itself regarded as illegitimate by a large part of the country. There was not much to hope for from the British, with or without the offer of Tobago.

Prussia offered rather better prospects since Frederick William had already been taught a lesson at Valmy and was unwilling to commit himself too heavily in the west when there might be more to be won or lost in Poland. He could also be tempted by

---

1. On this subject see the articles by A. Aulard in *La Révolution française,* 1890.

the offer to help himself to the territories of the petty rulers in western Germany, but he was in no hurry. If the 1793 campaign developed as well from the allied point of view as the victory of Neerwinden seemed to promise, he had everything to gain from staying on the winning side. If things turned out differently there would always be time for him – if not for Danton – to review the situation later. Spain was equally unresponsive and no doubt remembered the money that had been spent to no purpose in its attempt to save Louis XVI. Lebrun, who continued for a time to act as Foreign Minister even when he had been put under house arrest with the Girondins, was instructed to take advantage of any opportunity to open negotiations. None came.

In the case of Austria, Danton's only card was the fate of Marie Antoinette. Whether or not he would have been able to secure her release in return for a peace treaty was never put to the test, for her nephew, the Habsburg Emperor, was not prepared for any concessions. That was by no means the end of the matter, so far as Danton was concerned. His involvement in plans to save the queen's life has to be inferred from the fragmentary memoirs of his friend, the deputy Courtois, and not even from the memoirs themselves but from extracts made by historians before the original was destroyed.[2] If such evidence can be trusted, Courtois and Danton agreed to effect the queen's escape. When she refused to flee without her son, Danton exploded that her intention was to save not only her own life but the dynasty as well. Nevertheless he did not withdraw. In July he wrote to Courtois: 'The Commune will roar but that will be the chance for us to punish it and change those in power. Everyone will be on our side if we succeed; it will be the opposite if we fail; we shall have to defend ourselves and God knows what will happen. We must be prepared for anything.' If anything was planned, the scheme fell through when Marie Antoinette was transferred from her prison in the Temple to the Conciergerie on 2 August. Even then Danton may have tried to keep in contact with her.[3] There exists a letter to the queen, sent by the post, which said 'Citizen, you will place these words on your door, "Unity, indivisibility of the Republic, liberty, equality, fraternity or death." Signed, Danton.' This is presum-

2. A. Mathiez, *Autour de Danton*, Paris, 1926, Ch. 10.
3. C. Becker, 'A letter from Danton to Marie Antoinette', *American Historical Review*, 1921.

ably a forgery and even if genuine it could be innocuous. It would not have been in character for Danton to want to kill the queen when there was nothing to be gained by it. At the very least, saving her life might guarantee his, if things went wrong, and there could have been more positive rewards. To see all this as evidence of Danton's 'royalism' is to abdicate historical perspective for the hermetic mentality of 1793. Whatever his motives and his manoeuvres, nothing was actually achieved.

Danton's only diplomatic success was the signature of a treaty of friendship with Sweden. This was small beer at best and it was not even ratified since the Swedish Regent was intimidated by the presence of British and Russian fleets in the Baltic. From Danton's personal viewpoint the negotiations may not have been wholly fruitless if, as Barère claimed, he shared with the Swedish ambassador the money that the French had put up. On 28 June the Committee of Public Safety had persuaded the Convention to vote 4 million livres for diplomatic negotiations, so there was plenty of money to go round and his past embarrassments may not have cured Danton of his addiction to 'secret funds'.

Whatever personal compensations he may have picked up by the way, Danton's period of office on the Committee of Public Safety was a resounding political failure. He may well have been partially responsible for the collapse of the provincial revolt in most of the country, but Lyons drifted into open revolt, Marseilles and Bordeaux remained defiant and the war against the Vendée was going badly. The pursuit of a negotiated peace had been hopeless from the start and allied armies were pushing into France. It was not like Danton to back losers, but he had not much choice. The only alternative to the policy he pursued would have been to preach a revolutionary crusade, which would have meant radicalism at home and the kind of government interference with the economy that would have entrenched the commercial cities in their opposition to Paris. All this was to come in the summer of 1793, but as the result of popular pressure rather than government initiative. Most of his colleagues would have agreed with Danton's aims, if not necessarily with his methods, but his was the responsibility at a time when it was almost impossible for anyone to win. If victory was impossible without the radicals, defeat gave them their opportunity. The continuing French retreat and the usual rumours of treason kept everyone's nerves on edge and deprived the Committee of Public Safety of any moral authority. When a new constitution was hurriedly drafted, voted and accepted by most of the country, the collapse of the provincial revolt, except in three or four cities, meant that the Montagnards had no longer the same need to play the moderate card.

In the meantime, Danton was losing ground on other fronts. On 7 June he was criticised at the Jacobins for his poor attendance, one member alleging that he was not as revolutionary as he used to be. Desmoulins defended him and Danton presented his apology to the club a week later. This seems to be the only time that he spoke there between 2 April and 12 July. He blamed the pressure of work for his absence and said that he was worn out. He defended himself against the charge of moderation with the limp profession that he was always at work for the public good but had to pursue a policy of caution to win back the well-intentioned but weak. The Jacobins were fickle in their allegiance and their continuing support demanded constant attendance and participation in debate. Danton may well have felt that he had better things to do with his evenings, but revolutionary politics were becoming an increasingly full-time occupation, and influence over the club, once lost, was not easily regained.

The Committee of Public Safety also failed in its repeated attempts to get Bouchotte – and Vincent with him – out of the War Office. Bouchotte himself does not seem to have clung to office very tenaciously, but the War Office men were committed to the political survival of their patron. He handed in his resignation on 30 May but was saved by the insurrection on the following day, in which men from the War Office were said to have played an active part. On 14 June the committee tried again, proposing to replace him by Beauharnais, a noble. This was going too far; Vincent, Hanriot and Chabot protested and the committee was attacked in the Jacobins. Even Danton's friend, Legendre, said that it was worn out and Marat wrote that some (unnamed) members had neither life nor energy. Robespierre came to the rescue of the committee at the Jacobins. Though he personally preferred Bouchotte to Beauharnais, he prevented any discussion of their respective merits from extending to a general criticism of the work of the committee as a whole. Beauharnais thought it wiser to refuse the post, which was then accepted by Alexandre, whose military experience went back no further than 10 August

1792. Alexandre's appointment was defended by Fabre d'Eglantine but attacked by Legendre and Billaud-Varenne, and the Convention voted to retain Bouchotte.

Biron, the committee's man, had scarcely arrived in the Vendée before he quarrelled with Ronsin who had left the supply department for field service against the royalist rebels in the west. Bouchotte helped Ronsin by passing on to him all Biron's confidential criticisms of his subordinate – if that is not a misnomer for anyone as insubordinate as Ronsin. The committee stood by Biron and sent Gasparin, one of its members, to the Vendée to recall the commissioners sent there by the War Office. Gasparin allowed himself to be won over by the deputies already in the Vendée and Ronsin stayed where he was. Danton himself defended Ronsin and his associate, Rossignol, but out in the Vendée there was a growing polarisation between the War Office team on the one hand and Biron, Westermann and d'Eglantine's brother, Fabre-Fonds, on the other. The Vendée was the graveyard of military reputations, where any defeat was likely to bring charges of treason against those who had no strong political backing in Paris. When Westermann was routed at Châtillon on 2 June he was promptly arrested by local representatives on mission and sent to Paris for trial. Everything was going wrong for Danton and his men.

In spite of Robespierre, the Jacobins became increasingly critical of the Committee of Public Safety. Its powers, which had to be renewed by the Convention every month, expired on 10 July. On the 8th the club discussed it once again. Bourdon de l'Oise, who was soon to become Bouchotte's most bitter and persistent enemy, said that the committee was negligent. Chabot praised three of its members, Jeanbon Saint-André, Saint-Just and Couthon, but wanted to replace all the rest. Once again Robespierre defended it, calling Chabot a perfectionist and praising the committee as a whole. He was almost the only supporter it had left. In the Convention on 10 July it was attacked by Danton's friend, Desmoulins, angered by its refusal to make one of his aristocratic friends, Dillon, commander-in-chief on the northern front. Delacroix told Desmoulins he was not competent to criticise the committee since he hardly ever attended meetings of the Assembly and did not know what was going on. Drouet and Bentabole proposed reducing the committee, which had been enlarged on various occasions, to its original nine members, which included Danton and Delacroix. When a new committee was elected, however, Couthon, Saint-Just, Barère, Gasparin, Lindet, Jeanbon Saint-André and Hérault de Séchelles were retained, Thuriot and Prieur de la Marne were added and seven members were dismissed, including both Danton and Delacroix.

It is difficult to know what to make of this. Robespierre, who saw himself as the political mentor of the Assembly, did not intervene and that evening, at the Jacobins, turned angrily on members attacking Danton for having recommended a man of dubious loyalty to the navy minister. There is no evidence at all to suggest that he played any part in the dropping of Danton, which he probably regretted. Long afterwards, Barère said that Danton had favoured a reshuffle in the hope of eliminating his opponents. It is more likely that Danton was anxious to leave the committee, though naturally without a vote of censure round his neck. In a speech four days before the debate he had referred to the new assembly that would shortly be elected. If he expected the acceptance of the constitution to be followed by new elections he had everything to gain by exchanging membership of the discredited committee for the freedom of the back benches. Prieur de la Côte d'Or wrote, after the Revolution, that while he was in Normandy Danton's friend, Cheftel, told him that Danton intended to retire, get Robespierre elected to the committee, overwhelm it with new responsibilities and compromise it by inducing it to accept 50 million livres of secret funds.[4] This bears all the evidence of hindsight and is rather too neat to be convincing. Saint-André wrote that Danton told him several times that he thought the committee would be overwhelmed by its multifarious responsibilities, but if Danton was really planning to demolish Robespierre he must have been much more deficient in both gratitude and common sense than all the evidence suggests. Whether or not he let the deputies know that he did not wish to stand for re-election, he was probably not unhappy to be relieved of a situation that involved him in more routine work than suited his temperament and exposed him to continual criticism without allowing him to achieve any satisfactory results. His subsequent refusal to rejoin the committee strengthens the impression that he

4.   Quoted in G. Bouchard, *Prieur de la Côte d'Or*, Paris, 1946, p. 438.

was not sorry to leave it – in which case he was making a mistake. During the next few weeks things went from bad to worse. The military news was wholly black. In July the frontier fortresses of Condé and Valenciennes fell to the Austrians and the besieged garrison at Mainz surrendered to the Prussians. By executing the radical leader, Chalier, Lyons declared itself in open revolt. A counter-revolution in Toulon handed over France's second naval base and almost half the fleet to moderates of uncertain allegiance. Danton must have thought he had done well to get out of the limelight in time. On 13 July Marat was murdered by Charlotte Corday. Since she had been in touch with Girondin rebels before she left Normandy the republicans understandably, though wrongly, assumed that she was their agent. The discovery of the papers of a British spy suggested that the British Government was stooping to methods of warfare – currency speculation, the diversion of food supplies, arson and even assassination – that it would never have employed against a monarchist enemy.

The French reaction was one of increased ferocity against all opponents of the revolution, domestic and foreign. A new ruthlessness appeared on all sides, an increased determination to eradicate potential traitors and intensify the war effort at whatever cost to individual liberty and property. The death of Marat altered the situation in another way. The irascible journalist, although uninhibited in his criticism of almost everyone, had had no political ambition of his own and remained a loyal Montagnard. His immense popular following and his impressive knowledge of the skeletons in so many radical cupboards deterred anyone else from trying to build up a sansculotte following of his own. Once he was out of the way his would-be successors competed for the dead man's inheritance. Unlike him, they were eager to make careers outside the Montagnard family in the Convention. Roux and the Enragés, the first pretenders, were quickly eliminated. A powerful Jacobin deputation won back the Cordeliers and although Roux's own Section proved more loyal to him, he was arrested in September and the Enragés, who had never been particularly well organised or benefited from any central rallying-point, were soon reduced to silence.

Hébert, who had taken an active part in the campaign against Roux, intended to claim Marat's inheritance for himself. He now embarked on a political career of his own as the spokesman for a comparatively well-knit group that disposed of a formidable arsenal of revolutionary power. Pache and Hébert himself, with the rather unreliable support of the *procureur*, Chaumette, dominated the Commune and, subject to the fluctuating loyalties of the Sections, the city of Paris and its battalions of National Guards. Hébert's newspaper, the *Père Duchesne,* was a powerful propaganda weapon with a wide sansculotte readership. The War Office, safe in the hands of Bouchotte and Vincent, disposed of an immense amount of patronage, which extended beyond military and civilian jobs. Bouchotte supplied the troops with great quantities of suitable reading matter, which naturally included the *Père Duchesne* and the *Journal Universel,* edited by Pache's son-in-law, Audoin, who was also employed in the War Office. Bouchotte's agents were active all over the country, challenging the authority of the representatives on mission. Ronsin, with Bouchotte's backing, got his protégé, Rossignol, made commander-in-chief in the Vendée before Ronsin himself returned to Paris for higher things. The Cordelier club, under new management, provided the whole group with a rival forum to the Jacobins, where they could concert policy and make their views known to a wide public. Their advocacy of total war, the fiercer repression of domestic enemies, the purge of all nobles from the army, the introduction of price controls and their enforcement by a 'revolutionary army' of sansculottes whose main function would be to extract food from recalcitrant peasants, caught the popular mood.

There was nothing in the programme itself to frighten Danton. He had, as a matter of fact, proposed most of it himself at one time or another. What was more worrying was that the new Cordeliers were using the old tactics, slogans and policies to challenge the republican Establishment, as Danton had challenged the constitutional monarchists in the old days. No one was better placed than Danton himself to recognise the effectiveness of the techniques that had elevated him to his own position of revolutionary respectability. He would now make an unconvincing demagogue if he tried to beat his rivals at the old game. Probably he felt disinclined to try. It had been an exhausting year, culminating in the frustrating months on the Committee of Public Safety, and what he really wanted was to become an elder statesman of the revolution, taking things easy out of office and giving his colleagues the benefit of his experience from time to time.

He did not have this option, for the new Cordeliers singled him out as their main target, even reviving the old Girondin tactic of accusing him of corruption and collusion with Dumouriez. Their animosity kept him in the front line and left him with no alternative but to join the Montagnard fight to keep power concentrated in the Assembly and its committees.

After leaving the Committee of Public Safety he made a half-hearted attempt to revive his reputation as a radical, demanding death for anyone trying to negotiate with the rebels in Normandy, and the punishment of bishops who tried to prevent their clergy from marrying, and of administrators in the provinces who had declared for the Girondins, even if they had subsequently retracted. There was something to be said for freedom from responsibility, when it allowed him to advocate popular measures which were the exact opposite of those he had actually tried to implement. The Assembly elected him its president on 25 July, whether because he had recovered its confidence since leaving the Committee of Public Safety, or because he had never lost it. Hébert was unimpressed. At the Jacobins on 21 July, supported by Vincent, he insinuated that it would be straining charity to regard Danton and Delacroix as men who had merely lost their way. Since Hébert and his allies, instead of attacking Danton's present policies, preferred to rake up the old personal charges against him, it was clear that what they were after was not so much his defeat as his destruction.

Danton still disposed of some appreciable assets. One of his former clerks, Deforgues, was at the Foreign Office and another, Paré, took over the Interior in August — to the fury of Hébert who apparently wanted the job himself. On the whole, however, his political machine was a good deal the worse for wear. Losing the War Office meant that his military protégés would have an uphill fight. Legendre and Julien saved Westermann for the second time. He was acquitted of responsibility for the defeat at Châtillon and returned to the Vendée. This was all very well as far as it went, but Westermann had fallen behind Ronsin, whom Bouchotte promoted four times in a week, raising him from captain to general. In the meantime d'Espagnac lost his long fight against Cambon. His contracts were cancelled in July, despite Julien's efforts on his behalf, and both d'Espagnac and the former War Minister, Servan, were arrested. Delacroix managed to get d'Espagnac's dossier referred to a commission on speculation, of which Julien and Chabot were members, but the abbé's long career was finished. As his supporters and associates lost ground, Danton's strength was now confined to the Assembly. The Montagnards felt a good deal of affection for him as a man and he could always hope to win them over, in a crisis, by the sort of speech that had reversed the situation on 1 April. The Committee of Public Safety was well-disposed and he had no reason to regret the replacement of Gasparin by Robespierre towards the end of July. On the powerful Committee of General Security, which dealt with police matters, he could probably rely on Chabot and Julien.

There was no ground for alarm at the attacks of Hébert and Vincent, but Danton may well have felt that the revolution had changed its character, from a glorious – and profitable – adventure to something rather less attractive. He had won renown and made money and there was nothing in particular for him to aspire to now except the enjoyment of them both. Desmoulins, a weaker and more unpleasant man, had become thoroughly disillusioned with the situation that his own cruel and unscrupulous journalism had helped to produce. He wrote to his father on 10 August that he could not help thinking that the men who were being killed had children and fathers and he had begun to wonder whether he himself would survive a revolution where he saw nothing but ambition contending with ambition and cupidity with cupidity. With fewer doubts about his personal survival, for he always regarded himself as indestructible, Danton may have shared some of his friend's disillusionment. Since his future depended on the ability of the Convention to stand up to the pressure being brought to bear on it from outside, to understand the next stage in his career it is necessary to look at the political contest as a whole.

On 1 August Danton proposed that the Committee of Public Safety should be recognised as the provisional government of the republic and given 50 million livres of secret funds. To deflect any charge of personal ambition he said at the same time that he himself would not accept election to any committee of government. He had sounded opinion privately and been assured of the approval of some of the members of the committee, but when the Convention reacted unfavourably they drew back. Robespierre thought the motion too vague and likely to weaken the government rather than strengthen it. Jeanbon Saint-André, Barère and Couthon all said they would resign if the committee were given a budget of its own. Danton probably felt such ostentatious purity to be a reflection on his own personal record and he was understandably angry at being deserted in public by men who had encouraged him in private. He swore never to rejoin the committee and he was not without a certain shabby dignity when he continued:

> Last year, in the council of ministers, on my own responsibility, I took the measures needed to set things in motion and get the nation on the march to the frontier. I said to myself, 'Let them slander me; I foresee it, but it doesn't matter. Even if my good name is tarnished I will save freedom.'

His enemies were later to accuse him of introducing his motion in order to isolate and discredit the committee. He was quite used to saying one thing and meaning the opposite, but on this occasion he was probably quite sincere. He was aware of the danger from outside the Convention and throughout the rest of 1793 he was repeatedly to advocate strengthening parliamentary government. He had not been a Cordelier for nothing and the converted poacher knew a thing or two about gamekeeping. Vincent certainly took the point. At the Jacobins on 5 August he accused Danton and Delacroix of being conspirators, denounced the 'monstrous power' of the Committee of Public Safety and demanded that control over military appointments should be transferred to the War Office. Robespierre, in reply, attacked the new men who aspired to take the place of the revolutionary veterans. He named only the Enragés, Roux and Leclerc, but what he said had more relevance to Vincent. He then produced a eulogy of Danton, 'about whom no one has the right to raise the slightest reproach', that was specifically aimed at Vincent.

The new constitution had been made the subject of a referendum – it was approved by the great majority of those who chose to vote – and delegates from all over France assembled in Paris to bring the results of the referendum and to celebrate the anniversary of the fall of the Tuileries on 10 August. They were made honorary members of the Jacobins during their stay in Paris and their presence made the club more volatile and less responsive to the guidance of its usual leaders. The Cordeliers took advantage of the favourable conditions, the presence of the men from the provinces, the continuing military reverses and sansculotte agitation over food supplies, to step up their pressure on the Assembly. What was at issue was not measures but men. Danton had been violent enough on 12 August when he denounced any talk of an amnesty, demanded the arrest of suspects and suggested that the delegates from the provinces, on their return home, should be empowered to take a census of the crops and to raise the men for the new conscript army. The Cordeliers seem to have been thinking of a new 31 May that would intensify the Terror and transfer power into the hands of the ministers, a new revolutionary army and the local authorities – anyone, in fact, except the Assembly and its committees. With this went a personal attack on Danton. The *Père Duchesne* said that he and Paré were as thick as thieves, as friendly, in fact, as Danton had been with Dumouriez. Danton, at the Jacobins on 26 August, mildly invited Hébert to admit that his attacks were mistaken and went into a humiliating defence of his past financial transactions. Hébert contemptuously replied that he had been attacking the previous Committee of Public Safety as a whole, though he added that Danton had disappointed the *patriotes* in the Convention. Chabot, once a virtuoso of denunciation himself, said he was jeered and mocked everywhere and complained of a plot to destroy *patriotes* like himself and Danton.

By the end of August the situation was escaping from the control of the Montagnards. On the 28th the Jacobins decided to petition the Assembly to purge the upper ranks of the army – an implied criticism of the Committee of Public Safety. A member suggested that there should be fewer deputies and more commissioners from the ministers sent into the provinces. Hébert demanded the reorganisation of the executive itself and an honorary member from the provinces suggested asking the Convention whether or not it wanted to save the country. This was all too reminiscent of the scenes before the purge of the Girondins, with the public galleries abusing the members for their pusillanimity. On the following day Billaud-Varenne invited the Convention to set up a special commission to supervise the ministers. Robespierre, with Danton's support, fought off this attempt to create a rival to the Committee of Public Safety, but even he got a bad reception when he referred to the proposed body as a committee of denunciation. On 30 August at the Jacobins, Danton tried to swim with the tide, promising that 'if need be, the Mountain will make a third revolution, with the people'. Hébert had now won the Jacobins. On 2 September he persuaded them to vote to join the Sections and popular societies in a demand for the prompt trial of the Girondins, and was invited to draft the petition himself. Vincent called for the expulsion of Barère from the Committee of Public Safety.

The storm broke on the 4th. The news that the rebels at Toulon had handed over the ships there to the British and Spanish fleets and that the naval base with its great arsenal was in enemy hands, put the Committee of Public Safety at the mercy of its enemies. A workers' demonstration for higher wages, meeting outside the Hôtel de Ville, was captured by the Commune and persuaded to adjourn until the 5th, for a march on the Convention. That night the Jacobins began proceedings by sending two members to invite the demonstrators to meet at the club before moving on to the Assembly. Barère and Cambon were denounced. Robespierre defended Barère, but the club was in no mood to listen to him. On the 5th the Assembly was invaded by a crowd demanding the creation of a revolutionary army. Billaud-Varenne revived his motion for a new committee to supervise the executive and called for the arrest of suspects. Jeanbon Saint-André proposed referring these demands to the Committee of Public Safety, but Billaud insisted on their being voted on the spot. Danton now rose and he was perhaps as much surprised as gratified to be greeted by the applause of both the deputies and the crowd. It was the kind of situation that he knew how to handle. He began by conceding to Billaud an immediate vote on the creation of the revolutionary army. Pretending, as he had done in May, that the danger came not from popular insurrection but from the counter-revolution, he maintained that working men were debarred from regular attendance at the Sections by their need to earn a living. He therefore proposed to substitute for the nightly meetings of the Sections, two meetings per week, with payment for attendance to those in need. He then went on to demand that every citizen be given a musket and that at least 100 million livres be voted to accelerate arms production. In conclusion, he endorsed a previous proposal to multiply the revolutionary tribunal and intensify repression. His peroration, 'Homage to you, sublime people . . .', brought him the kind of triumph he had not known for a long time: 'universal applause from all parts of the hall; repeated shouts of *Vive la République!* All the deputies and spectators rise to their feet; some raise their hands, others wave their hats; universal enthusiasm'. Danton had done it again. He had deflected criticism of the government into enthusiasm for national defence and turned the whole atmosphere of the meeting. He presumably realised that all the gunsmiths of France were inadequate to equip the conscript army that had been voted in the previous month, and nothing more was heard of the proposal to give everyone a musket. Vincent and his friends quickly realised that limiting the meetings of the Sections broke their continuity, and treating them as a form of public assistance weakened the hold of the militant minorities, but the crowd had seen the proposal in a different light and it was the kind of motion that no one could oppose. Danton could still teach his opponents a trick or two in the handling of revolutionary situations.

When the deputation from the Jacobins arrived the mood had changed and the pressure on the government had eased. Robespierre, who was in the chair, could now be evasive and the Committee of Public Safety escaped with no commitment beyond the creation of the revolutionary army. That night Billaud was elected president, in succession to Robespierre, and the following day he and Collot d'Herbois were added to the committee, which put an end to his opposition. Danton was elected too. When he declined, the Convention over-ruled him, but on 9 September he reminded his colleagues of his oath never to rejoin the committee and forced them to accept his refusal. He was probably comparing his success, as an independent member, on the 5th with his frustration in June and July, but he was taking a bigger gamble than he may have realised.

Although the immediate threat to the government had been averted, it had to make further concessions, notably over price controls and the arrest of suspects, in the following weeks. Its radical opponents were not defeated yet and their hands were strengthened by the new legislation. The revolutionary committees of the Sections, after being purged by the Commune, were empowered to detain anyone indefinitely without trial. The Commune also controlled the issue of *certificats de civisme,* which were necessary for any form of public employment. Fabre d'Eglantine, in a private note, was particularly scathing about the opportunities this afforded for gerrymandering.

> The honest man who knows what work means is scandalized by what he sees in the ministries, especially those of war and the navy, and in the Commune and the Department . . . What sort of people get certificates? The Ronsins, Jourdans, Maillards, Vincents, bankrupts, gambling-house keepers, brigands and cut-throats . . . The Commune is running a racket in this department.[5]

Vincent was still on the offensive. On 18 September he persuaded the Cordeliers to petition the Assembly to prevent representatives on mission from interfering with the agents of the ministers. Two days later he gave the members of the club his views on the past and present members of the Committee of Public Safety and once again attacked Danton as the tool of Dumouriez. Vincent was a violent man and he obviously thought that things were going his way. According to a denunciation made in the spring of 1794, he was a member of a noisy dinner party in September 1793 when the guests, all drunk, boasted of having drunk out of counter-revolutionary skulls.

> Little by little, criticisms of the Convention became more bitter. They objected because it had not organized the executive council in accordance with the constitution. [i.e. had new ministers elected, who would be independent of the Committee of Public Safety]. They said they knew how to force it to do so, with the help of the revolutionary army; that a new 31 May was needed; that they would cut the throats of all the traitors in the Convention; they added that there were only 12 to 15 *patriotes* amongst the deputies.[6]

Vincent was no doubt very drunk, but he was none the less dangerous for that.

On 24 and 25 September the Committee of Public Safety was attacked in the Convention. This seems to have been a combined assault by deputies disgruntled at being recalled from their missions, radicals who wanted price controls and others demanding the immediate trial of the Girondins and the queen. Danton was

5. Archives Nationales, F[7] 4434.
6. Archives Nationales, AF II 49.

away ill but Robespierre defied the committee's critics and won a vote of confidence. From this time onwards the government, although it had to accept price controls and sacrifice Marie Antoinette and the Girondins, gradually won control of the situation. On 3 October Robespierre had to concede the trial of the queen to Billaud but he stopped him from getting a formal vote on the prosecution of the Girondins, which would have identified their defenders and exposed them to proscription. The radicals were still powerful enough to impose Bouchotte's nominee, who was naturally Ronsin, as commander of the revolutionary army, when the Committee of Public Safety would have preferred Hanriot, but the tide was beginning to run against them. On 8 October Danton's old Section, which had long since escaped from his control, was frustrated when it attempted to have Robert tried on a capital charge of hoarding rum, and the Convention refused to lift his parliamentary immunity. That night Vincent was booed into silence at the Jacobins after his Section had illegally arrested the editor of the club's newspaper, who had criticised Bouchotte. The government scored a decisive victory with the decree of 10 October which extended revolutionary government for the duration of the war — in other words, suspended the application of the new constitution indefinitely — and expressly placed ministers, generals and the administration as a whole under the control of the Committee of Public Safety. The Cordeliers were still powerful and Hébert retained a considerable personal following in the Jacobins, but their attempt to capture the machinery of revolutionary government had failed.

Danton had played no part in all this since he had been ill from about the middle of September. In his last speech to the Assembly, on 13 September, he denounced the committee responsible for army contracts. There was perhaps more to this than met the eye. Chabot and Basire, when in November they exposed the speculators with whom they had been associated, claimed to have been told by Delaunay, a deputy and an associate of Julien, that Danton and Thuriot had originally been involved with Delaunay but had left him, apparently soon after 13 September.[7] Their plan had been to intimidate speculators against the revolutionary paper currency, to hold them to ransom and force them to pay in bills

7. Letters of Chabot to Danton on 28 November and 2 December. Archives Nationales, F[7] 4434.

of exchange drawn on foreign banks, a convenient combination of patriotism and self-interest. There is no other evidence that Danton was involved in anything of the kind and Basire and especially Chabot are thoroughly unreliable witnesses. If they were telling the truth, there is no means of knowing why Danton broke with Delaunay, but it could possibly explain his motion against the committee on war contracts. The sequel to his proposal may have disconcerted him. True to his general policy, he proposed to empower the Committee of Public Safety to nominate the members of all other committees. When this was adopted by the Assembly, the Committee of Public Safety promptly renewed that of General Security – which Danton had specifically commended – getting rid of Chabot, Basire and Julien. Some of its new members were, or were to become, bitter enemies of Danton.

On 12 October Danton applied for and received permission to retire to Arcis to convalesce. Leave of absence of this kind was quite exceptional and his motives have been the subject of much speculation. The straightforward explanation is that he was tired and ill, wanted to avoid the distressing spectacle of the judicial murder of Marie Antoinette and the Girondins and to indulge his love of idleness and the country. It may well be true. It is also possible that he was somehow involved in the attempt to clean up corruption that followed the purge of the Committee of General Security. The new committee searched Julien's apartment, which frightened Chabot into burning his own papers. Men exposed by Danton's motion to change the committee on war contracts may have set out to punish or blackmail him. Writing to Danton from gaol at the end of 1793, Chabot said that Delaunay had told him, 'Danton was one of us; he left us and you can see how we are hounding him'. In another letter he said that Delaunay's associate, Benoît, claimed to have been close to Danton and to have persuaded him to retire to the country.[8] This may or may not have something to do with the cryptic comment by Pereira to Amar, a member of the new Committee of General Security, on 7 October: 'Danton's stock has been falling for the past fortnight'.[9] Whatever all this may mean, if it means anything at all, it is

8. A. Mathiez, *Un procès de corruption sous la Terreur. L'affaire de la Compagnie des Indes.* Paris, 1920, pp. 80, 94, 97, 103.
9. J. Herissay, *Cet excellent M. Danton*, Paris, 1960, p. 358.

difficult to see why Danton should have felt safer away from Paris, where he could hope to influence the course of events. An even more unlikely explanation of his absence is Mathiez's suggestion that he was intimidated by the denunciation of the gaolbird, Comte, to the effect that Danton had been mixed up in intrigues with royalist agents in Normandy. When Comte told this to Hérault de Séchelles, Hérault promptly had him arrested. It took more than that to frighten Danton. Contemporary views are no more helpful. Lacretelle, in a history of the revolution published a few years after the events it described, said that Robespierre advised Danton to retire and promised to let him know when to return. Danton's school-friend, Béon, on the other hand, said that Robespierre reproached him for deserting the political battlefield. They were probably both guessing.

Whatever his motives, Danton was experienced enough to know what he was risking. Revolutionary reputations were tender plants in need of constant care. He might be satisfied that the radical attack was running out of steam, but his own reputation was likely to suffer in his absence and he would have an uphill fight, on his return, to recover his influence over the Jacobins and the Convention. Perhaps he no longer cared and hoped that he would never need to return.

IX The End of a Career

Danton remained at Arcis-sur-Aube from mid-October until 18 November. He kept to his house at first, but once his recovery was complete he began to visit his friends and inspect the property he had acquired in the neighbourhood. He also took advantage of his presence in Arcis to buy more land, but on a very small scale, his purchases not adding up to more than 6,000 livres. He seems to have enjoyed himself, leading the life of a prosperous and sociable gentleman farmer, but there was no escaping from the revolution. His sons repeated to Villiaumé the story that, early in November, a neighbour greeted him with the good news that his old enemies, the Girondins, had been convicted and executed. 'You wretch, you call that good news! . . . You say they were factious. Aren't we all? We deserve death as much as the Girondins and we shall suffer the same fate one after the other.' Whatever the accuracy of this particular story, it probably indicates his real state of mind. Garat, the former Minister of the Interior, wrote in his memoirs that when he talked to Danton towards the end of 1793 the revolutionary leader said to him, with the Girondins in mind, 'I offered them peace a score of times but they refused it. They refused to believe me so that they could preserve the right to destroy me. They are the people who drove us into the arms of *sans-culottisme*, which consumed them, which will consume us all and consume itself.'[1] There was a good deal of truth in this, but Danton's own conduct had provided them with a tempting target.

Legend has it that one of his rural excursions was interrupted by the arrival of his nephew, Mergez, sent by friends in Paris to urge him to return since Robespierre was after his blood. This is a good example of the myths that bedevil his whole career, since Mergez was in an Austrian gaol at the time and if Robespierre was thinking of Danton, it was more likely to have been in the hope of enlisting his help.[2] No one knows why he came back to

1.   Garat, *Mémoires,* Paris, 1862, p. 317.
2.   E. Campagnac, 'Deux agents de Danton, Recordain et Mergez', *Annales historiques de la Révolution française,* 1953.

Paris when he did, but it is likely enough that he looked back nostalgically on Arcis and his plans for life as a country gentleman, when he said goodbye to his mother and his friends and took the road to the frenetic capital. He certainly returned a rather different man. From now onwards he made little attempt to disguise his moderate policies behind a façade of verbal violence and there were to be no more of his volcanic eruptions until he found himself in the dock.

While he had been away from Paris, revolutionary politics had become more embittered and more personalised. Levasseur, returning from the front in mid-November, found the Assembly 'so changed that my head swam and I could scarcely recognise my colleagues . . . In the place of the Mountain, formerly so compact and united, I found a swarm of rival factions that dared not fight each other in the open but waged underground war.' The underground warriors themselves had only a vague and confused idea of what was going on. They were all fighting in the dark against real or imaginary enemies. The historian is at an even greater disadvantage since much of what was said was never put on paper and a good deal of what was written down was prudently destroyed. Political issues were entangled in a multiplicity of personal feuds, and allies in one context could be enemies in another. Allegiances changed; opponents were bought off or possibly blackmailed into support. Corruption cut across politics, confusing everything. The air was thick with accusations of treason, some of which were possibly intended seriously and may even have been true. The written evidence for all this is fragmentary at best and often deliberately misleading or genuinely mistaken. Danton had always enjoyed swimming in such turbid waters and the man who called public opinion a whore was not going to endanger the present in order to explain himself for the benefit of posterity. Despite all the uncertainty and complexity, and the probability of misreading some of the signs, one has to plunge into the thick of the confusion if one is even to try to understand where Danton stood and what he was attempting to do.

The failure of the extremists' attack on the revolutionary government in the autumn still left them entrenched in their positions of power and in possession of the initiative. Throughout the period of Danton's retirement in Arcis, Hébert had kept up a continuous attack on him and his supporters, with the approval of

many if not most of the Jacobins. On 20 October the club pet-
itioned the Convention to protect the *Père Duchesne* from harass-
ment by Dufourny, the president of the Paris Department. A week
later it adopted Hébert's motion that the trial of the Girondins
should be curtailed and sentence pronounced within twenty-four
hours. On 8 November Hébert denounced Fréron, the friend of
Danton and Desmoulins, for his conduct on mission and secured
the appointment of a commission to investigate both Fréron and
his colleague, Barras. Lavaux, the editor of the Jacobin newspaper,
the *Journal de la Montagne,* who had presumed to criticise
Vincent, was bullied into resignation and replaced by Hébert's
nominee. When Chabot, Basire and Thuriot protested in the
Assembly that the Terror was getting out of control, and won the
right of any accused deputy to a hearing before his colleagues,
Hébert attacked them in the Jacobins and the Convention reversed
its vote. On 13 November Hébert accused Delacroix of having
plundered Belgium in the previous spring. This brought the attack very close to Danton himself. Thuriot was expelled from the
Jacobins on the same day. Three days later Hébert persuaded the
club to demand the recall from their mission in Normandy of
Danton's friends Delacroix and Legendre. When the Jacobins
decided on a purge of their members Hébert was elected to the
purge committee. On 21 November he told the club that he had
met Danton in Paris that morning, reminded the members of
rumours that Danton had fled the country and invited him to come
to the club for a 'fraternal' explanation.

Hébert's sustained offensive had gone almost unopposed by
Danton's friends and allies. Fréron, Delacroix and Legendre were
all away and Fabre and Desmoulins said nothing. Bourdon de
l'Oise was carrying on a one-man vendetta against Bouchotte in
the Convention, but this seems to have been a private war of his
own. In the Jacobins, only Dufourny stood up to Hébert, and his
allegiance is far from clear. He was the enemy of Danton's
enemies, but also the sharpest critic of Chabot and Basire, recent
converts to the virtues of moderation.

Robespierre, so far as one can see, believed that the military
victories of the autumn meant that the Republic could no longer
be overthrown by force of arms and the way was open for a
gradual return to constitutional government. He was also convinced that the allies, and especially Pitt, were concentrating their

efforts on destroying the revolution by intrigue and corruption, setting the republicans against each other by means of agents who passed themselves off as good revolutionaries. Prompted by a secret denunciation that Fabre had made in October, Robespierre thought he had identified Proli, Desfieux, Dubuisson and Pereira as some of these foreign agents, who were misleading honest but gullible men like Hébert. His immediate task was therefore to protect the veterans of the revolution against each other's suspicions and to destroy the counter-revolutionaries who were setting them against each other. On both personal and political grounds, he reacted violently against the campaign attacking the Christian religion that developed in November, culminating in the Festival of Reason in Notre Dame on the 10th and the Commune's closure of all Paris churches on the 23rd. Proli and his friends – not eminent for either their personal sanctity or a passionate interest in theology – were involved in this campaign which Robespierre saw as exactly the kind of measure that was designed to create opposition while having a specious revolutionary appeal to the more naïve radicals. It may well have been dechristianisation that convinced him that the time had come for the revolutionary government to assert itself. He had a good memory and he no doubt recalled Danton's warning, almost exactly a year before, about the need to respect the strength of religious feeling in the provinces. He may not have invited Danton's support now but he certainly received it and he seemed to welcome it.

A very different reason for Danton's return from Arcis may have been provided by the plot denounced to the Committee of General Security by Chabot and Basire on 15 and 16 November.[3] Chabot maintained that certain deputies and their backers, notably Delaunay, Julien and d'Espagnac, had profited from their political influence to blackmail bankers and trading companies by threatening them with punitive legislation. Their most recent coup had been to falsify, in return for a substantial bribe, the text of a decree recently voted, for the winding up of the East India Company. His information about all this was circumstantial and almost certainly rested on a basis of fact. More vaguely and less plausibly, he spiced the financial intrigue with a second, political,

3. N. Hampson, 'François Chabot and his plot', *Transactions of the Royal Historical Society*, London, 1976, pp. 1–14.

plot to discredit those revolutionary leaders who could not be bought, by a systematic campaign of calumny. Corruption and defamation were thus two branches of a single plot, organised by Benoît on behalf of the royalist Baron de Batz, whose real intention was to destroy the Convention by turning its members against each other. This was close enough to Robespierre's suspicions to strike him as plausible and it apparently allowed Chabot to insinuate that the defamation plot involved Hébert, who had been hounding him at the Jacobins. He himself, of course, had only pretended to take part in the plot as yet another of his many services to the revolution. Basire said nothing about the political side of things – which was perhaps an invention of Chabot's – and could only describe the earliest stages of the financial racketeering. Both he and Chabot, without themselves involving Danton, claimed that Delaunay and Benoît had done so. Basire referred to Danton's support, in July, for the speculation in revolutionary currency, while Chabot said he had been told that Danton, Delacroix, Panis and Robert had parted company with the speculators, apparently in September. This could have had something to do with Robert's difficulties about his rum. The financial side of the 'revelations' sounds plausible enough and no more sinister than a good many of Danton's other activities. What made it potentially lethal were the political trimmings that Chabot included, such as his allegation that Benoît, twice sent on confidential missions by Danton when he was Minister of Justice, was a royalist agent. Chabot, before he was arrested with the men he had denounced, gave a full account of his story to Courtois, no doubt for onward transmission to Danton, and it may have been a letter from Courtois that brought Danton back to Paris. If Chabot, as seems likely, was trying to save his own neck by revelations that had some foundation in fact, Danton may well have been implicated in the original speculation. That was the kind of evidence that could be made to disappear by tactful intervention in the right places, and Basire's charges against Danton were, in fact, subsequently edited out of his declaration. There was enough here to suggest that the best place for Danton was Paris.

Chabot had exonerated from participation in the East India Company affair all those whose political support he might require. As he presented it, the affair involved only Benoît, Delaunay, Batz and Julien, with himself and Basire as virtuous double agents.

What he appeared not to know was that the fraudulent version of the decree included the signature of Fabre d'Eglantine. Fabre had originally thwarted those who were harrying the company, presumably to raise his price, but had almost certainly made a deal with them. Chabot's exposure therefore put him in mortal danger. Danton, who was not personally involved, may have been unaware of this, at least initially.

About the time that Danton returned to Paris, on 21 November, Robespierre opened an attack on the extremists, in the Jacobins. He criticised Hébert, although without naming him, denounced dechristianisation as part of a counter-revolutionary foreign plot, and had Proli and his quartet expelled from the club. This marked an abrupt departure from his policy throughout the autumn, when he had sometimes criticised measures, but not the motives of the men who advocated them. Danton was soon active in the Convention, attacking the dechristianisers and on every occasion calling for the concentration of power in the hands of the Committee of Public Safety. His open support for moderation probably corresponded to Robespierre's private opinion, although Robespierre limited himself to cautious hints in public. On 22 November Danton demanded 'that we be sparing of human blood'. Two days later, when the Convention was discussing the law that was to put the whole of revolutionary government under the control of the committees of Public Safety and General Security, it was Danton who suggested the creation of 'national agents', to be chosen and dismissed at will by the Committee of Public Safety, who should supervise local government on behalf of the central authority. This was to undermine the power of Chaumette and the Paris Commune. On the 26th Danton persuaded the Assembly to refer to the Committee of Public Safety all the denunciations that representatives on mission were launching against each other. He followed this up with an attack on 'anti-religious masquerades' and called for a prompt report on Chabot's plot.

We must pursue traitors everywhere, whatever their disguise, but we must be careful to distinguish between error and crime. The will of the people is that Terror should be the order of the day, but that it should be directed against the real enemies of the Republic and against them alone. It is not the people's will that the man whose only fault is a lack of revolutionary vigour should be treated as though he were guilty.

This was to repeat the protest of Chabot, Basire and Thuriot against the indiscriminate extension of the Terror and Danton was accused, as they had been, of the heinous offence of advocating clemency. He defended himself against this as well as he could, though without the oratorical violence with which he had concealed his moderate policies in the past. Later in the debate he took advantage of a petition for the organisation of primary education to call for educational, as well as administrative centralisation. Leaving aside the question of schools, he proposed the introduction of national festivals. 'If Greece had its Olympic Games, France too will celebrate its *jours sansculottides.* The people will have festivals where it will offer up incense to the Supreme Being, Nature's master, for it was never our intention to destroy superstition so that atheism could reign in its place.' This sounded very much like offering up incense to Robespierre, who was to inaugurate just such a festival in the following year.

Fabre d'Eglantine, too, was playing a Robespierrist tune. Although he was not a member of the Committee of General Security, he and Amar, who was, were put in charge of the interrogation of Chabot and Delaunay. After going through Chabot's denunciation Fabre produced a skilful 'summary' that neatly transformed its content, insinuating that the men accused by Chabot were also responsible for dechristianisation and repeatedly incriminating Chaumette, whom Chabot had not even mentioned.[4] Running through it all was a good deal of none-too-subtle flattery of Robespierre.

So far Danton had had a fairly easy passage in the Convention and he seems to have kept away from the Jacobins. At the club, Hébert had become curiously silent. Soon after Chabot's denunciation he and Chaumette were summoned to appear before the Committee of General Security. Chaumette told the Commune on 22 November that Robespierre had defended them and they had been cleared of all charges, but they may have been advised to keep quiet. When Danton did appear at the Jacobins, on 3 December it was not Hébert, but the relatively obscure Coupé who

4. Reprinted in A. Mathiez, *Un procès de corruption sous la Terreur: l'affaire de la Compagnie des Indes,* Paris, 1920, pp. 145–67.

accused him of moderation. When Danton rose to reply there were signs of hostility. Instead of challenging his critics, Danton struck an almost pathetic note.

> Have I lost the appearance of a free man? Am I not the same man who was at your side in times of crisis? Am I not the man you have often embraced as your friend, the man who was to die with you? Am I not the man who has been overwhelmed by persecution? I have been one of the most fearless defenders of Marat. I will conjure up the shade of the People's Friend in my justification. You will be astonished, when I reveal my private life to you, to see that the colossal fortune your enemies and mine have credited to me, is reduced to the little property I have always owned. I defy the ill-intentioned to prove me guilty of any crime.

He apparently delivered this with some passion and impetuosity, but it was feeble stuff, and so was his melodramatic invitation to the president to appoint his most irreconcilable enemies to a commission that would examine the charges against him.

At this point Robespierre brought up his heavy artillery to Danton's support. Understandably embarrassed by the fact that within four months Robespierre was to charge him with every crime in the counter-revolutionary calendar, Robespierrist historians have tried to argue that their hero damned Danton with faint praise. Danton's partisans, equally unhappy, have attacked the speech as insincere. Neither view stands up to serious examination. Robespierre began by listing the charges against Danton, of fleeing the country, aspiring to become Regent to Louis XVII and so on, to demonstrate their palpable absurdity. He admitted that he had sometimes disagreed with Danton and even scrutinised his conduct with anger, but asserted that the differences between them were a matter of temperament.

> Danton wants to be judged and rightly so. Judge me too. Let them come forward, these men who are better *patriotes* than us. I'll wager that they are nobles, men of privilege. You'll find a marquis amongst them and that will give you the measure of these grandiloquent accusers.

(The last shaft was aimed at the former marquis, Maribon-

Montaut, who was trying to atone for his social origins by the violence of his revolutionary opinions.) It would have taken a brave man to accept Robespierre's challenge and nothing more was heard of the commission to investigate Danton. The president gave him a fraternal accolade and even the Cordeliers expunged the charges against him that they had entered in their minutes, and did it so thoroughly that Robinet was unable to read them. After this session Danton, like Hébert, relapsed into relative silence. During the next three weeks he spoke only briefly in the Assembly and twice in the Jacobins, on relatively minor and uncontroversial issues. This was the very period when the so-called 'Dantonists' launched an attack on extremism that was to broaden out into a challenge to revolutionary government itself. The question of how far Danton approved of this campaign, or even directed it from behind the scenes, therefore merits careful examination.

At first sight the evidence for his leadership of those whom their opponents called *Indulgents* is overwhelming. Garat, who claimed to have met Danton several times at this period, said that he returned from Arcis with a plan for the restoration of normal political life, the return to the Assembly of those Girondins who were still alive, the amendment of the constitution, the restoration of peace and the abolition of economic controls. To bring this about, he proposed to prepare the ground by a press campaign, to build up a party in the Convention, isolate the extremists on the Committee of Public Safety – Collot d'Herbois, Billaud-Varenne and Saint-Just – and win over Barère and Robespierre. He would constantly press for the concentration of more and more powers in the hands of the committee, either to satisfy its ambition or to discredit it as tyrannical, and then induce the Convention to replace some of the members of both governing committees.[5] There may be an element of hindsight in this but it sounds reasonably plausible.

Danton's friend, Courtois, recorded in his notes that Danton was working with the *Indulgents* and that he moderated some of the rasher passages in the newspaper that Desmoulins was soon to write. According to Courtois, Danton compared Hébert, Ronsin and Momoro to 'so much internal wind that a misplaced sense of

5. Garat, *op. cit.*, pp. 317–19.

decorum prevents a man from blowing off'.[6] That has a genuine ring about it and Courtois would never have thought it up for himself. Claretie, in the nineteenth century, asserted that Westermann, recalled to Paris after helping to defeat the rebels in the Vendée, proposed to Danton that he should carry out a coup d'état and Danton refused, saying that he would a hundred times rather be guillotined than guillotine others. Courtois also mentioned this offer by Westermann, and Villiaumé said he heard it from Rousselin, a young protégé of Danton's, but both of them date it to the period immediately before Danton's trial and it looks as though Claretie got the date wrong.

Disregarding the Westermann business, this constitutes a fair amount of support for the not very surprising proposition that Danton was aware of what his friends were doing, but some contemporaries thought differently. Levasseur, in his *Observations présentées au Comité de Salut Public* (rather surprisingly preserved amongst the papers of the Hébertists), denounced Fabre as the leader of a faction that included Philippeaux, Bourdon de l'Oise, and Desmoulins (Fabre's dupe), but did not mention Danton.[7] In his memoirs he wrote that Danton remained for a long time outside Fabre's faction and only turned against the Committee of Public Safety after Fabre's arrest, on 12 January 1794. Villain d'Aubigny, who had been a business associate of Danton and Legendre in 1791 and subsequently attached himself to Saint-Just, denounced Fabre, Bourdon and Thuriot while retaining his affection for Danton.[8] Hébert, when he attacked the *Indulgents* in the Jacobins on 21 December, said that the only two men who still retained his confidence were Robespierre and Danton.

This may merely mean that Danton confided in his friends and succeeded in bluffing everyone else. What mattered at the time was what people believed. So far as one can make this out, Robespierre was very slow to dissociate himself from the *Indulgent* campaign, and after he had done so, both he and others remained on good terms with Danton. It is quite likely that the *Indulgents*

6. Robinet, 'Notes et souvenirs de Courtois', *La Révolution française*, 1887.
7. Archives Nationales, W 76.
8. Herlaut, 'La vie politique de Villain d'Aubigny', *Annales historiques de la Révolution française*, 1934; L. Jacob, 'Robespierre et Villain d'Aubigny', *id.*, 1950; Villain d'Aubigny, *Principaux événements pour et contre la Révolution*, Paris, an III.

themselves were not entirely in agreement. Fabre had his own reasons for wanting to overthrow the revolutionary government in time to hush up the East India Company scandal. Danton had less need to be in a hurry and would prefer to work through the Committee of Public Safety if he could.

The campaign started in earnest when Desmoulins published the first issue of his *Vieux Cordelier* on 5 December. The title was well chosen to remind his readers of the contrast between the veterans of the old club and the new men who were now using the Cordeliers' name. The first number claimed that Pitt and the extremists in France were scheming to bring about Danton's downfall but had been thwarted by Robespierre's defence of him in the Jacobins. The second issue, on 10 December, consisted largely of an attack on dechristianisation. Robespierre had been shown the proofs and he borrowed some of Desmoulins' language in a speech at the Jacobins a couple of days later. In the meantime, Bourdon de l'Oise had extended his regular denunciations of Bouchotte, in the Convention, to include the Paris Commune and the revolutionary army. Philippeaux, back from the Vendée, published a couple of fierce pamphlets, blaming the poor showing of the republicans on the incompetence of the Committee of Public Safety. These various activities may have represented a convergence of dissatisfactions rather than an orchestrated campaign, but it would not look like that to the government.

On 12 December, when the powers of the Committee of Public Safety came up for renewal, Bourdon and Merlin de Thionville carried a motion that some – perhaps half – of its members should be replaced. This was the high-water mark of the campaign and it is certainly odd that the committee seems to have made no attempt to defend itself. It was a very obscure deputy, Jay de Saint-Foy, who on the 13th persuaded the Convention to leave the committee as it was. Robespierre may have welcomed the idea of replacing one or two of his colleagues, such as Billaud-Varenne. He certainly does not seem to have regarded the motion as any kind of 'Dantonist' attack on the government, for on the 14th he delivered a very warm eulogy of Desmoulins who passed the Jacobin scrutiny committee, along with Danton and Fabre. Chabot, who was surprisingly in touch with current affairs for one who was supposed to be *incommunicado,* wrote a couple of letters to Danton, on 10 and 14 December, which were addressed to him as a member of the Committee of Public Safety.[9] This could have been a mere slip, though he was unlikely to have made the same mistake twice. More probably it was an echo of the unsuccessful manoeuvre to change the committee and put Danton on it. If Chabot, in his cell, knew what was going on, it is most unlikely that Robespierre was in the dark. He was generally alert enough to every political move and if he continued, not merely to protect his old allies, but to co-operate with them, it is reasonable to suppose that he had no very strong objections to what they were trying to do.

Despite their failure to change the composition of the committee, the *Indulgents* – whoever they were – kept up the pressure. The *Vieux Cordelier* No. 3, on 15 December, compared the state of the republic unfavourably with that of Rome under the tyranny of its emperors. Desmoulins praised Robespierre and Philippeaux, attacked Vincent, Bouchotte and (without naming him) Collot and implied that the Committee of Public Safety was abusing its powers. Two days later, Fabre persuaded the Convention itself to order the arrest of Vincent, instead of proceeding through the Committee of General Security, as was customary. Other deputies had Ronsin and Maillard arrested as well. Couthon, who generally followed Robespierre's lead, instead of objecting to this encroachment on the powers of the governing committees, joined in the condemnation of these 'dangerous men'. That night Fabre reminded the Jacobins that Vincent's sponsor when he applied for membership of the society had been Hébert. On the 20th the *Vieux Cordelier* called for the establishment of a committee of clemency to liberate genuine revolutionaries who had been arrested by mistake – or by the wrong faction – and Robespierre proposed something very similar to the Assembly. During these hectic three weeks Danton had said virtually nothing. If *Indulgence* was the programme of a 'Dantonist' faction, Robespierre looked a better Dantonist than he was.

Everything was transformed by the return, on 21 December, of Collot d'Herbois, a member of the Committee of Public Safety who had been at Lyons, where he and Ronsin had presided over the brutal and ferocious repression of the counter-revolutionaries. Ronsin had been arrested almost as soon as he got back to Paris

9. Archives Nationales, F7 4434.

and Collot had no intention of sharing his fate. Going straight to the Jacobins, he was immediately cleared by the purge committee and invited by Hébert to give an account of his experiences at Lyons. This gave him a suitable opportunity to complain of the change that had come over the Jacobins in his absence and to attack those responsible for the arrest of Ronsin. Hébert, who had been practically silent for the past month, put his moustache back on again, in the words of Desmoulins, and resumed his old rôle, denouncing Philippeaux and Desmoulins and demanding the expulsion of Bourdon from the club. It was at this point – when he was certainly not making any concessions to the *Indulgents* – that he expressed his confidence in Robespierre and Danton. The Jacobins, perhaps rather relieved to escape from the monochromatic moderation that Robespierre had been foisting on them, voted their confidence in Vincent and Ronsin and invited Fabre, Bourdon and Desmoulins to come and justify their conduct. There were now two opposing factions, with their extremists protected by one of the members of the Committee of Public Safety. If Robespierre persisted in his support for the *Indulgents* he risked splitting the committee and bringing down the revolutionary government. On 23 December, at the Jacobins, he tried to put himself above the battle and, without attacking individuals, attempted to dissuade Philippeaux from incriminating the committee and to discourage Momoro from playing with the idea of a new 31 May. Whether or not they came to any understanding, Robespierre, Danton and Collot all behaved as though they were in agreement, condemning faction and coming to each other's support. Danton, for the first time, began to express an opinion about the party wrangling. He took up the same neutral position as Robespierre and was himself supported by Couthon when he demanded an investigation into Philippeaux's attack on the committee.

Robespierre's disengagement from the moderates was not achieved without one of his rare political humiliations. When he complained on 26 December that the committee to review the cases of those allegedly arrested in error had been chosen in his absence, Billaud-Varenne replied that the whole idea – Robespierre's idea – had been a stupid one in the first place, and persuaded the Assembly to have the committee abolished. Despite the tacit non-aggression pact between Robespierre, Collot and Danton, the two factions intensified their attacks on each other in the Jacobins. On 5 January 1794 Collot was criticising Philippeaux and Desmoulins, but in fairly moderate terms, when Hébert sprang up shouting 'Justice!' and waving a copy of the *Vieux Cordelier* No. 5 in which Desmoulins accused him of drawing huge subsidies from Bouchotte. Danton then intervened as a neutral arbiter. He expressed no particular views about Philippeaux, defended Ronsin, as he had always done, and told Hébert to wait for time to vindicate him. Robespierre followed, in a similar vein, praising both Collot and Danton.

Whether he was genuinely detached from the faction fight or merely presenting a public impression of impartiality, Danton's position seemed secure enough. He was not involved in the mud-slinging between Desmoulins and Hébert. If the *Indulgents* had won, they would presumably have turned to him as their leader. If they lost, he had avoided compromising himself and might be able to cover their retreat. It is difficult to be sure where anyone stood, but the evidence scarcely supports those historians who maintained that Danton was a mere shell of his former self, meekly trailing in Robespierre's wake. On 7 January Philippeaux presented twenty-six charges against Vincent and Ronsin to the Convention, took up Desmoulins' accusations against Bouchotte and demanded the reorganisation of the War Ministry. Danton agreed with him that the ministers should be denied access to the Treasury and even proposed their abolition, but as usual he suggested referring everything to the Committee of Public Safety. He took no part in the increasingly violent quarrels in the Jacobins, where he did not speak for over two months, leaving the defence of Desmoulins to Robespierre.

His position changed with the discovery of evidence that seemed to prove that Fabre d'Eglantine had been the accomplice of Delaunay in the falsification of the decree for the liquidation of the East India Company. Robespierre, whom Fabre had been leading by the nose, turned on him with understandable fury at the Jacobins on 8 January and Fabre was arrested four days later. Robespierre now began to revise his views of the *Indulgent* campaign that Fabre had apparently organised and to see both *Indulgents* and Cordeliers as opponents of the revolution. Whether from motives of personal friendship or because he was afraid of what Fabre might reveal in an attempt to save himself, Danton, who had not made any attempt to help Desmoulins, came to his support. On 13 January, when Amar asked the Convention to lift Fabre's parliamentary immunity, Danton made a clumsy attempt to rescue him. On the flimsy pretext that the Assembly had not much business to occupy its time, he suggested that the accused should be given a hearing at the Bar of the House instead of being interrogated by the Committee of General Security. This earned him the stinging rebuke from Billaud-Varenne, 'woe to the man who sat next to him [Fabre] if he is still his dupe'. That day Desmoulins' wife wrote a desperate letter to her friend, on mission at Toulon:

> Come back Fréron, come back quickly. There is no time to lose. Bring with you all the old Cordeliers you can find, we need them badly . . . [Robespierre] has seen that when he didn't think and act in accordance with the views of certain people he was not all-powerful. Marius [Danton] is not listened to any more; he is losing heart and becoming weak. Déglantine is arrested and in the Luxembourg; he is accused of very serious charges.[10]

There is some evidence that Danton and Robespierre met about this time and that they quarrelled. On both personal and political grounds Robespierre had good reason to prefer Danton to the dangerous Billaud-Varenne, with whom he had crossed swords more than once, but if the price of Danton's support was the rescue of the hopelessly compromised Fabre, there was nothing he could do.

The next two months were a time of suppressed tension, with everyone playing for time and waiting for the storm to break. Sooner or later the government would have to put Fabre on trial. Vincent and Ronsin could not be left indefinitely in gaol either. The Cordeliers – the new ones, not Lucile Desmoulins' old ones – were agitating for their release. They had protectors in the Committee of General Security who were unlikely to agree to a trial that would risk splitting the government and setting off a popular insurrection in their favour. If they were liberated they were not the kind of men to remain quiet but would take the warpath against their persecutors. Robespierre had managed to enforce

10. Quoted in J. Clardie, *Camille Desmoulins, Lucile Desmoulins*, Paris, 1875, pp. 296–7.

silence on the Jacobins by persuading them to debate the crimes of the British Government. Heinous as these no doubt were, they were not inexhaustible and the club became restive. Desmoulins complained that 'no one was permitted to write' and suspended publication of his newspaper. The strain was too much for Robespierre who took to his bed for a month. Danton appears to have abandoned the Jacobins. He was unusually assiduous in his attendance at the Convention where he spoke frequently, but generally on minor matters.

On 24 January Desmoulins complained to the Assembly that his father-in-law had been arrested on a trumped-up pretext. Danton, while objecting to deputies claiming special treatment for their relatives and careful to emphasise his acceptance of such repression as might be necessary, used the occasion to revive Robespierre's projected committee of clemency and had his proposal referred to the Committee of Public Safety. When Voulland, of the Committee of General Security, told the deputies that the only evidence against Vincent and Ronsin consisted of the unsupported allegations of Philippeaux, and proposed their release, Danton seconded him. Conveniently ignoring the fact that they were accused only of political heresy while Fabre was charged with corruption, Danton drew a false parallel between the two cases, enunciated the principle that revolutionary veterans should not be lightly suspected and announced that he would defend Fabre for the same reasons that led him to support the two extremists. If this was intended as some sort of olive branch towards the Cordeliers it had no effect. Once at liberty, Vincent and Ronsin began a campaign for vengeance, carrying Hébert with them and threatening a new insurrection.

Danton continued to support the Committee of Public Safety, to which he wanted all proposed legislation referred. When the abolition of slavery was voted on 4 February, his was the cool voice that invited the governing committee to define the ways in which emancipation could be effected with least danger of social upheaval. Three days later he supported the efforts of Lindet, the most humane member of the Committee of Public Safety, to save the councillors of Conches who had been ordered before the revolutionary tribunal by Danton's friends, Delacroix and Legendre. Towards the end of February, however, he began to sound a new note. When Lacoste, of the Committee of General Security, secured the Assembly's automatic approval of the dismissal and arrest of the members of a military court, Danton objected.

We vote without knowing what we are doing, taking mere reports on trust. I declare that I could not follow what was said or exercise my functions as a political juror. It is time the Convention resumed its rightful place and only decided when in full possession of the facts. The nation must not be lost because we are cowardly, weak or dumb. This is only the preface to my political opinion; I will enlarge on it in due course.

The Convention followed his lead and reversed its previous motion. Most of the deputies had probably had enough of the Terror. They were not eager for martyrdom and not disposed to take any avoidable risks, but they might follow a resolute lead and call to order the two committees which were becoming increasingly high-handed in their treatment of the other members of the Assembly. But if Danton hoped to inspire his colleagues with the courage to challenge the government, he went about it very cautiously. Perhaps he recognised that so long as the Cordeliers were threatening a new 31 May, the deputies would look to the committees for their protection.

On 26 February Saint-Just introduced his 'ventôse decrees'. These were the unexpected outcome of the discussions about a committee of clemency. Saint-Just had been instructed to report on those in gaol on political charges. In a speech directed mainly against the Indulgents he proposed the liberation of arrested patriotes but demanded that those who were confirmed as 'enemies of the people' should have their property confiscated and be deported at the end of the war. Danton secured an amendment to this, to the effect that the revolutionary committees of the Sections, responsible for the arrest of suspects, should be required to provide the Committee of General Security with a list of their members and their activities throughout the revolution, so that the committee might eliminate faux patriotes à bonnet rouge.

A fortnight later this warning against ultra-revolutionaries seemed to have been taken to heart by the government. On 13 March Saint-Just denounced the existence of a new plot. His carefully chosen abstractions could have applied to either the extremists or the Indulgents or to both, but it was Hébert, Vincent, Ronsin, Momoro and a curious assortment of their alleged associates who were arrested that night. Six days later the Paris Commune at last brought itself to congratulate the Convention on destroying a movement in which some of its other members as well as Hébert had probably been involved. Ruhl, of the Committee of General Security, who was in the chair, reproached the Commune for its delay. Danton, enigmatic to the end, suggested that Ruhl had been too severe. Ruhl offered to reply and invited Danton to take his place in the meantime. Danton refused, praising Ruhl, who said to him, 'You must take the sense of what I said and judge my words indulgently, as I would yours, if you yourself made a mistake'. He meant what he said; within a fortnight he was to warn Danton that a warrant was out for his arrest. It was the end of Danton's career in the Assembly and the frequent applause for his exchange of compliments with Ruhl suggested that he was still popular there. He himself was confident that no one would dare to attack him.

With the execution of the leading Cordeliers on 24 March the Convention was relieved of any threat from Paris. If they had the will and the courage, the deputies could now reassert their control over the committees that ruled in their name and they could look to Danton for a lead. But on 19 March the Assembly had voted for the trial of Fabre, Chabot, Basire and Delaunay. The immediate question was what Danton would do to save Fabre – or what the committees feared that he might do.

X The End of a Life

Danton was aware that he had implacable enemies within the two governing committees. He knew that Vadier had said of him, 'That fat stuffed turbot, we'll gut him too'. He had reciprocated the delicacy of this sentiment, when speaking to the painter David, whom he told that, if he felt his life in danger, he would become 'more cruel than a cannibal' and promising to eat Vadier's brains and shit in his skull.[1] Vadier meant what he said and Danton did not. Whatever the feelings of the members of the Committee of General Security, on a matter of such importance they would take their cue from the Committee of Public Safety; Lavictomterie claimed that his own committee was taken completely by surprise when the Committee of Public Safety announced its intention to proceed against Danton. Courtois said that Billaud-Varenne and Barère, of the Committee of Public Safety, as well as Vadier and Amar of General Security, were out for Danton's blood. Villain d'Aubigny, who knew all the men concerned, said that Billaud and Saint-Just were always calling Danton a traitor, although they did not believe anything of the kind.[2] Danton himself had a mistaken confidence in his invulnerability. He had never failed to extricate himself from difficult situations in the past. If one can trust Barras, he told the two committees that Philippeaux's criticisms of the conduct of the war in the Vendée were fully justified. Vadier, Amar and Barère replied that Philippeaux was Danton's own mouthpiece. This provoked a furious quarrel, presumably about the end of 1793, and Danton threatened to denounce 'the committee' (it is not clear which) to the Convention.[3]

With the Committee of Public Safety divided, everything depended on Robespierre. He was far from being a dictator and he could not impose his own will on the committee, but he enjoyed immense prestige in the Assembly and especially in the Jacobin

1. Robinet, 'Notes et souvenirs de Courtois', *La Révolution Française*, 1887, p. 813.
2. Villain d'Aubigny, *Principaux événements pour et contre la révolution*, Paris, an III, p. 2.
3. Barras, *Mémoires* (Eng. trans.), London, 1895, Vol. I, pp. 193–4.

Club. If he openly quarrelled with Billaud and Saint-Just over Danton's fate, the Committee of Public Safety would be torn apart and the combined force of Robespierre's reputation and Danton's oratory would probably command a majority in the Assembly. No one was likely to risk such a showdown. Robespierre was demonstrably reluctant to sacrifice Danton. He had however, come to believe that the *Indulgent* campaign, with which he had for a time identified himself, had been a disguised attack on revolutionary government, and he began to denounce both extremists and moderates, particularly the latter. In an undelivered speech, probably drafted in mid or late January 1794 and perhaps censored by his colleagues, he attacked a whole string of moderates, including Fabre, Philippeaux, Bourdon, Desmoulins and Westermann, and made a passing reference to 'the indolent and proud *patriote,* eager for both repose and fame, who was hoodwinked by Fabre into cowardly inactivity or led astray into a labyrinth of false and pusillanimous policies'. Nevertheless he seems to have been genuinely attached to Danton. Billaud-Varenne complained that when he first attacked Danton, Robespierre, in a furious rage, accused him of wanting to destroy the best *patriotes.* Apart from his personal feelings, he was too experienced a politician not to realise that the death of Danton would leave him dangerously isolated. Courtois thought that Robespierre feared Danton's rivalry and hoped to force him to become his prisoner and supporter.[4] A curious anonymous manuscript in the Archives Nationales, *Who then was Robespierre?,* claims that Danton was threatened by the two committees. 'Robespierre, perplexed, came to his rescue but soon, either because he realised that he and Danton would not be strong enough to overthrow the committees or because he feared that praise of Danton would give credit to any attack that Danton might make on him, Robespierre joined the committees to overthrow Danton.'[5] It looks as though Robespierre hoped to avoid proscribing anyone and wanted to deal with the factions by political means, browbeating both sides into silence and leaving them unharmed. The task was probably beyond him in any case and during his month's illness the situation escaped from his control, with the Cordeliers breaking away and calling openly for an insurrection.

4. Robinet, *op. cit.,* p. 811.
5. Archives Nationales, 29 AP 78.

Something like this is suggested by a letter that Couthon, whose views generally echoed Robespierre's, wrote to his constituents on 8 March. He assured them that intrigues in Paris would come to nothing. Without mentioning any names, he referred to the activities of moderate and violent factions. The former,

> continually at odds with their consciences, use underground means to do all they can to obstruct revolutionary measures, lest they themselves should be the victims. In this way, although they perhaps do not *mean* to conspire, these corrupted men [*hommes gâtés*] become *in fact* veritable counter-revolutionaries. That is where men are led by the first step on the road to crime. It will be sufficient, I hope, to draw public attention to these *Messieurs,* whose cowardice is the least of their faults, in order to foil all their plans.[6]

Five days later Saint-Just made the speech that served as the prelude to the arrest of the Cordeliers. Most of it, however, was directed against the moderates and the only man named was Chabot. By the middle of March the two committees had probably decided to destroy the East India Company speculators who had been awaiting trial for nearly four months. This posed no judicial problem since there was plenty of evidence against them. They did, however, include Fabre and the question was whether Danton would agree to sacrifice his friend and political ally. If he did, the execution of Fabre and Chabot would balance the destruction of the Cordeliers, leaving the governing committees unchallengeable and Danton isolated but unharmed. Danton was not the man to sacrifice friendship on the altar of *raison d'état,* even if the *état* in question was the immaculate Republic. This was probably what Robespierre found so hard to understand. If Danton chose to put his formidable lungs at Fabre's disposal he might swing the Assembly and overthrow the government. The alternative – to turn a clear case of corruption into a major political crisis by putting Danton in the dock with Fabre, when there was no evidence linking him with the East India Company business – looked equally dangerous. This was the frightening dilemma that faced the committees during the second half of March and it tried their nerves to breaking-point.

6. F. Mège, *La correspondance de Georges Couthon,* Paris, 1872, p. 306.

On 16 March Amar at last reported on the East India Company affair. His speech lasted three hours but the report in the *Moniteur* occupies only one page and there is no means of knowing all that he said. He was immediately criticised by both Billaud and Robespierre for concealing the political implications of the case and his report was referred back to the Committee of Public Safety. It was most unusual for members of one committee to object to the proposals of the other, but it is impossible to say exactly what Billaud and Robespierre had in mind. Two days later it was not the Committee of Public Safety but Amar again who introduced a revised report. Although this was very similar to his first effort and included only the vaguest reference to the political motives of the accused, it seems to have been accepted without debate. This meant that Fabre and Chabot would be tried in the near future and the question of what to do about Danton could not be postponed much longer.

From now onwards the trail becomes hard to follow. When Couthon told his constituents, on 18 March, that the East India Company men were to be brought to trial, together with Hérault de Séchelles of the Committee of Public Safety (nominally arrested for protecting an *émigré*), he did not imply that there were to be any more victims. 'We can breathe at last; the political horizon is clear and the skies are calm. The plots reveal themselves and the plotters are arrested.'[7] The enigmatic Bourdon de l'Oise chose this moment to renew his attacks on the government. On the 19th he tried to implicate the Paris Commune and his old enemy, Bouchotte, in the insurrectionary plans of the Cordeliers. On the following day he secured the arrest of the committees' leading police agent, Héron, a vote that Robespierre promptly had reversed. If anyone was creating trouble it was not Danton but Bourdon, who was to survive all the purges until 1797 when he was deported as a royalist. His survival in April 1794 is something of a mystery. Couthon promptly changed his tune. Coming to the rescue of Héron, he told the deputies that 'the conspiracy that has been denounced is not the only one . . . One of these days the Committee of Public Safety will identify to you the men who make up the moderates'. Robespierre too accused the (unidentified) moderates of trying to exploit the overthrow of the

7. F. Mège, *op. cit.*, p. 283. Mège dates this letter 28 *nivôse* (17 January) which must be wrong. The most likely date is 28 *ventôse* (18 March).

Cordeliers and implied that their tactic was to take the judgement of the conspiracy (presumably that of Fabre and Chabot) out of the hands of the committees and the revolutionary tribunal, presumably by referring it to the Convention itself. On the following night he warned the Jacobins that the moderate faction was still at work. 'The time to expose it will come; that moment is not far off.' Couthon wrote on the 22nd that he and Robespierre had begun to attack those trying to profit from the fall of the Hébertists. 'Within a few days there will be a report that will finish off the job. There are some people who should not speak so loudly.' On the 24th he once more mentioned the coming report: 'We have decided to strip off all the veils and expose in their nakedness all the men who have betrayed the public trust.'

Contemporaries got the impression that the committees decided to cut the Gordian knot about 22 March. There were certainly rumours to this effect which Danton heard and disbelieved. His young protégé, Rousselin, told Villiaumé long afterwards that one of the jurors on the revolutionary tribunal, Vilate, said to him early in *germinal*, 'We must have the heads of Danton, Camille Desmoulins and Philippeaux within a week'.[8] The first of *germinal* was 21 March. The deputy, Thibaudeau, claimed in his memoirs that he warned Danton five or six days before his arrest – i.e. on 24–25 March.[9] Robespierre's follower, Arthur, wrote to the public prosecutor on the 28th, offering to give evidence in 'the affair of Danton, Lacroix [Delacroix] etc.'.[10] This was a bold move when the men in question had not even been arrested. Robespierre's brother wrote privately to him from Toulon on 5 April, having just heard of the execution of Hébert, to suggest that the real plotters were 'the two big D—— and D—— of the Convention', which presumably meant Danton and Desmoulins, since his contemporaries generally referred to Delacroix as 'Lacroix'.[11]

If Robespierre appeared to be giving way, he was still hesitating. He had two or three private meetings with Danton, the

8. M. N. Villiaumé, *Histoire de la Révolution française*, Paris, 1850, Vol. IV, p. 36.

9. *Mémoires sur la Convention et le Directoire*, Paris, 1824, Vol. I, p. 60.

10. Archives Nationales, W 342.

11. G. Michon, *Correspondance de Maximilien et d'Augustin Robespierre*, Paris, 1926, Vol. I, p. 272.

last of them as late as 29 March. The best-authenticated of these was arranged by d'Aubigny and took place at the house of Humbert, the brother of Robespierre's former landlord, a fortnight before Danton's death, i.e. about 22 March.[12] The existence of this meeting was confirmed in 1795 by Legendre who was present, together with Panis, Deforgues, the Foreign Minister, and others. Danton complained that Billaud and Saint-Just had turned Robespierre against him. He appealed to Robespierre to support him in uniting the *patriotes* and limiting the scope of repression. Robespierre, at first very cold, appeared to be won over and the two men embraced each other. Tissot, a well-informed contemporary historian, a relative of one of the deputies and an eyewitness of the scene in the Convention on 31 March when Danton's arrest was announced, claimed that the two men met at Charenton, on the outskirts of Paris, at some unspecified date, when Robespierre denied that the Committee of Public Safety harboured any animosity against Danton.[13] Both Robespierre and Saint-Just referred to what Robespierre called a 'final' meeting in the presence of the deputy, Laignelot. Barras was told by Laignelot that Robespierre said Danton's conduct in Belgium had perhaps not been above reproach, but seemed to throw most of the blame on Delacroix.[14] Robespierre himself said that Danton affected to weep and dissociated himself from Desmoulins, whose misconduct he said was due to his private vices, whatever that meant. The deputy, Lecointre, was perhaps referring to this meeting when he quoted Billaud as having said that the day before Robespierre consented to abandon Danton, the two men met twelve miles from Paris (which would seem to rule out Charenton) and returned in the same coach.[15]

Whatever the precise details, it is clear that Robespierre's consent to the proscription of Danton was belated and reluctant. Perhaps because he knew of Robespierre's hesitation, Danton refused to take the initiative and attack the committees. For this there were both tactical and psychological reasons. He said to Courtois, 'They want to force me to unmask them. I shall have to

12. D'Aubigny, *op. cit.*, p. 49 note 1.
13. P.-F. Tissot, *Histoire de la Révolution française*, Paris, 1839, Vol. V, pp. 125-7.
14. Barras, *op. cit.*, Vol. I, p. 191.
15. L. Lecointre, *Les crimes des sept membres des anciens comités de salut public et de sûreté générale*, Paris, an III, p. 25.

reveal the full turpitude of their policies and Monsieur Billaud will be exposed at last, in spite of all his Jansenist hypocrisy.'[16] There was a good deal to be said for remaining on the defensive when an attack was likely to unite the committees. Besides, Danton had perhaps ceased to care. When Rousselin warned him of his coming arrest he was both incredulous and world-weary. 'My life is not worth living. I am tired of humanity.' He refused to try to escape with the much-quoted phrase, 'You can't take your country with you on the soles of your shoes'. The longer the rumours persisted the more convinced he would feel that nothing was going to happen.

It is said that Danton was thrown off his guard by Robespierre's friendliness towards him just before his arrest. Riouffe, a fellow-prisoner, wrote that he heard Danton say as much when he was in gaol. Courtois told the same story and it was repeated by Desmoulins, if we can believe the well-informed contemporary pamphlet, *The trial and punishment of Camille Desmoulins*.[17] This lends credibility to Villiaumé's melodramatic story of how Marat's sister warned Danton of his impending arrest and urged him to take the offensive. He was reluctant to do so, on the ground that he himself would have to proscribe Billaud and Robespierre. When Mlle Marat convinced him that he had no option, since he could not rely on a fair trial if he himself was arrested, he went to the Convention intending to denounce them. He there saw Robespierre in friendly conversation with Desmoulins, who assured Danton that there was nothing in the rumours. He therefore did nothing – and was arrested that night.[18] Ruault, one of the editors of the *Moniteur,* had heard a somewhat similar tale. He wrote to his brother that Danton's popularity had revived since he and Desmoulins had identified themselves with opposition to the Terror, at the end of 1793. Ruault believed that Danton, Desmoulins and Hérault de Séchelles planned to de-nounce the Committee of Public Safety to the Convention on the day before Danton was arrested.[19] This cannot be wholly true since Hérault was already under arrest. If Danton himself had any such intention, something must have happened that made

16. Charavay catalogue, Bibliothèque Nationale, △ 40153.
17. Archives Nationales, AD I 108.
18. Villiaumé, *op. cit.,* Vol. IV, p. 41.
19. N. Ruault, *Gazette d'un Parisien sous la Révolution,* Paris, 1976, pp. 362–4.

him change his mind. Even if Mlle Marat got her facts right, this need not imply deliberate deception on Robespierre's part. He may not have finally given way until the joint meeting of the two committees on the night of 30–31 March that led to the arrest of Danton, Desmoulins, Delacroix and Philippeaux at two in the morning.

The meeting itself seems to have been dramatic enough. Saint-Just presented the report mentioned by Couthon, which he proposed to read to the Convention on the following morning, denouncing Danton to his face and demanding his arrest. When Saint-Just's colleagues rejected this as far too dangerous a gamble and insisted that the four men must be arrested first, he threw his hat in the fire and Vadier and Amar were just in time to prevent the report following it. Robespierre at first supported Saint-Just but was silenced when Vadier told him, 'You can risk being guillotined if you like, but I don't intend to'.[20] When the decision was taken, Lindet refused to sign the warrant and both he and Ruhl warned Danton. Carnot claimed later that he too had opposed the arrest, but he signed with the others.[21]

Once Danton's arrest was decided no one had any further choice. It would be a fight to the death, with the revolutionary tribunal as the arena. Robespierre, having accepted, if not exactly willed the end, did not shrink from the means. Saint-Just showed him the draft of his report and Robespierre began by making brief comments: 'Delete,', 'Rectify', 'Explain'. Warming to his task, he went on to formulate charges of his own against the four 'conspirators', laying particular emphasis on Danton and trying to plead extenuating circumstances in the case of Desmoulins.[22] Saint-Just was to rely so much on these notes, to which he made only minor amendments, that it is hard to imagine what he could have put in his own draft. This was the only 'evidence' that was to be offered against Danton. Nothing is known of the content of Saint-Just's original report, but Robespierre's notes have survived. They make curious reading. Danton was charged with

20. P-A. Taschereau-Fargues, *A Maximilien Robespierre aux Enfers*, Paris an III, pp. 15–16. Courtois (Robinet, *op. cit.*, p. 809) refers to the same incident.

21. Carnot, *Réponse . . . au rapport fait sur le 18 fructidor*, London, 1799, pp. 168–9.

22. A. Mathiez, *Etudes sur Robespierre*, Paris, 1958, Chapter VI.

everything in general – except corruption – and of nothing very much in particular. Robespierre accused him of various political heresies such as his former support for Mirabeau, the constitutional monarchists, Orleans and the Girondins, his opposition to the execution of the king and to the coup d'état of 31 May 1793. Criticism of this kind could have been directed against almost anyone and it was rather more applicable to some of Robespierre's colleagues on the two committees than to Danton. He did accuse Danton of one or two specifically counter-revolutionary offences – helping Dumouriez to save the Prussian army and intriguing with him in the spring of 1793 to overthrow the Convention – but there was surprisingly little of this and he produced no evidence of Danton's guilt. He seasoned his charges with a good deal of character-assassination, the proof of Danton's 'black and un-grateful soul'. Long-suppressed irritants came out into the open. 'Danton laughed at the word *vertu* and said there was no *vertu* more substantial than what he showed to his wife every night.' Losing all sense of proportion, Robespierre hinted that Danton had stopped him from having Brissot murdered during the September massacres and claimed that Danton's motion about the abolition of slavery was merely intended to deprive France of her colonies. Saint-Just left out some of these more injudicious accu-sations. The charge against Robespierre is not that Danton was innocent. He was, in fact, guilty of far more than Robespierre suspected. Robespierre, however, had known what he knew for a long time, certainly since the previous December when he had dismissed as absurd the evidence he now produced as conclusive. Perhaps he had changed his mind or perhaps he felt that the overriding need to save the revolution justified him in presenting the changing demands of the tactical situation as moral absolutes.

The first problem facing the committees was to secure the assent of the Convention. Danton was personally popular, if not respected, and there were many who might feel themselves threatened if they allowed him to fall, including the president, Tallien, who had been recalled by the Committee of Public Safety from his mission to Bordeaux. It is impossible to know just what happened on the morning of 31 March since newspaper editors had learned to trim their reporting to suit current political orthodoxy. The committees were invited to come to the Assembly, a bad tactical mistake if the intention was to challenge them. Legendre, claiming that he believed Danton to be as innocent as he was himself, said that the arrested men were victims of personal animosity and should be given a hearing by their colleagues. He was opposed by Fayau, an obscure deputy who had already attacked Danton during the winter, but Legendre apparently got some shouts of support. Robespierre then entered and rounded on Legendre and anyone else who maintained that Danton was a privileged person. Legendre's brief defiance was over. No one had supported him at the rostrum, whatever they had cried from the safe anonymity of their seats. He excused himself and from that time onwards was profuse in his praise of the government and pious horror at the mention of conspirators. Barère, who seconded Robespierre, admitted that 'there has been talk of dictatorship; the word has been ringing in my ears for the past quarter of an hour'. The Assembly was now sufficiently cowed for Saint-Just to read his report in silence and secure a unanimous vote for the trial of the four accused. The committees had won the first round without much difficulty.

All that remained was to have the conspirators convicted. For this purpose Danton and his three fellow-deputies had their case tacked on to that of Fabre, Chabot and the East India Company racketeers. The trial ought not to have presented too serious a problem. The committees imposed the same tight censorship that they had enforced during the trial of Hébert and kept proceedings out of the press. The president of the revolutionary tribunal, Herman, and Fouquier-Tinville the public prosecutor, had given proof enough of their reliability and of their efficiency. Fouquier, it was true, had once claimed a distant relationship to Desmoulins when he wrote to ask him for a job, and he owed his position to Danton, but he had enough republican *vertu* to put gratitude in its proper place. Making doubly sure, the government reinforced him with Fleuriot-Lescot, a faithful follower of Robespierre. They may still have had some doubts, if Villiaumé is right in saying that orders were given to arrest both Herman and Fouquier when they expressed uncertainty about their ability to obtain the right verdict. Villiaumé claimed to have seen a note, in Collot's hand, dated 2 April, the day the trial opened, countermanding this order. It was important for the committees to maintain the fiction that Danton and the rest had merely been accused by the Assembly, given a fair trial and only convicted when their guilt had been proved to the satisfaction of an impartial court. To have arrested the court's two chief officers on the day the trial began would have exposed this shabby pretence from the start. Amar, Vadier, Voulland and David, of the Committee of General Security, were in constant attendance at the court to ensure that nothing went wrong.

Fouquier was reliable enough but he had his problems. That methodical man was happy to destroy anyone the government wanted convicted but he liked the process of judicial murder to proceed in an orderly fashion and this was a distressingly irregular case. On 26 March he had given orders for the trial of Fabre, Chabot and company, but not of Danton.[23] He had prepared this case with his usual care, supplementing the evidence from Amar's report with his own notes on the interrogation of Chabot and Delaunay. He had drawn up a list of witnesses to appear 'in the affair of Chabot, Basire, Fabre, Delaunay and others, for 2 April'.[24] There was a small irregularity here, for Lulier, who appeared among the witnesses, was included with the accused in Fouquier's file of notes on Amar's report – and Lulier had not even been arrested. That could be – and was – rectified during the trial. Everything suggests that Fouquier was taken completely by surprise when Danton, Desmoulins, Delacroix and Philippeaux were added to his clients. He was presumably told nothing until their arrest on 31 March and the trial was due to begin two days later. No one supplied him with any evidence and all he had to go on was Saint-Just's report. He did compile a list of *pièces à rechercher* but he never used them and possibly never had time to assemble them. In the case of ordinary prisoners, the lack of evidence would not have mattered very much, but to accuse a man like Danton on vague political charges was positively to invite him to launch a counter-attack for which Fouquier was not prepared. His main hope lay in the ruling, introduced at the time of the Girondin trial, that after three days the jury could declare themselves satisfied and cut the trial short. They might be three difficult days but time was on Fouquier's side.

The committees succeeded in denying to both contemporaries and posterity any accurate knowledge of what happened. The press was muzzled and the Jacobins were told only as much as

23. Archives Nationales, W 342.
24. Archives Nationales, W 173.

was good for them. The official minutes describe the form of the
trial but not its content. The *Bulletin of the Revolutionary Tribunal* was edited by men associated with the court, in conformity
with what they assumed to be political orthodoxy. It devoted
several issues to what it at first described as 'the affair of Chabot
and accomplices' and later altered to 'the affair of Danton, Lacroix
etc.'. The *Bulletin* is the main source for what happened but it
leaves out most of what concerned Danton and gives no indication
of the reactions of the public. A juror, Topino-Lebrun, made
notes during the trial. These were destroyed in the Paris Commune of 1871 but extracts from them were used by Claretie in
1887 and Robinet published his version of Topino's manuscript.
Further evidence was produced when Fouquier himself was put
on trial in 1795 and a fair proportion of the proceedings amounted
to a retrial of Danton.[25] Fouquier got a fairer hearing than he
had given to others, but the evidence produced against him has
obviously to be handled with caution. The sources for Danton's
trial are so unsatisfactory that one cannot even be sure how many
jurors there were. The official minutes record seven names and
this is the number given by all Danton's biographers. Fouquier,
however, in the notes that he took during the trial, crossed off
thirteen jurors as recording their verdict on each of the questions
put to them. Dufourny, who was present throughout, said that
four or five were hesitant and the remaining eight went to consult
Robespierre every morning.[26] He may have been guessing about
the consultations with Robespierre but he could presumably count
up to thirteen.

   The trial began on 2 April and attracted an enormous crowd
that overflowed from the courtroom and stretched in a long queue
through the neighbouring streets. Michelet asserted that, from
time to time, Danton's voice could be heard across the Seine.
Despite the precautions of the committee, there was going to be a
good deal of publicity, even if it took the form of rumours passed
along the crowd. Proceedings opened with a recital of the names,
ages and addresses of the accused. According to some editions of

   25.   Archives Nationales, W 501, reprinted in Buchez and Roux, *Histoire
parlementaire de la Révolution française*, Paris, 1834–8, Vol. XXXIV, pp. 233
et seq.
   26.   Archives Nationales, W 173, for Fouquier's notes, W 501 for
Dufourny's evidence.

the *Bulletin,* Danton, when his turn came, gave his address as 'soon, in oblivion, but my name will be in history's Pantheon', which suggests that he had not much doubt about the verdict.[27] Fouquier then filled in time by having the reports of Amar and Saint-Just read out. This was legitimate enough in Danton's case since it was all the evidence he had. According to the *Bulletin,* 'these different charges were supported by written evidence and by witnesses'. This is rather delicately put. There is no record of any written evidence; many witnesses had been called, but Cambon was the only one heard. Dufourny, despite his insistence, was not allowed to give evidence. From the garbled accounts that have survived it is impossible to be sure when any particular incident occurred, but this may have been the moment when Danton said, 'Provided they let us speak at length I am sure of routing my accusers and if the French people is what it ought to be, I shall have to ask it to pardon them'. Amar, Vadier and the observers from the Committee of General Security cannot have found that particular prospect very reassuring. At some stage or other, Lulier, who had been called as a witness, was added to the accused.[28] Westermann was also accused during the course of the trial, which added to Fouquier's difficulties. Westermann insisted on being officially charged and when Herman objected that this was an unnecessary formality, Danton interjected, 'Our whole presence here is only a formality'.

The rest of the day was devoted to the financial scandals. Cambon spoke at length and dispassionately. He was hard on his old adversary, d'Espagnac, and on Julien, but confined himself to matters of fact. Danton took advantage of his presence to ask Cambon if he believed him to be guilty. The *Bulletin* ignores this. Topino-Lebrun noted Danton's comment: 'Look! He laughs. Note down that he laughs.' This is more convincing than the claim by Danton's friends, Pâris and d'Aubigny, at Fouquier's trial, that Cambon defended Danton so warmly that the audience was moved and the court became anxious. The cross-examination of Cambon and the defence of the men accused of corruption took

---

27. This is printed in the edition of the *Bulletin* in the Bibliothèque Nationale, but not in that in the John Rylands Library in Manchester.
28. The version of the *Bulletin* printed in Buchez and Roux (Vol. XXXII, pp. 107 *et seq.*) says Lulier was *removed* from the accused. This is probably a misprint: *rayé du* has been substituted for *rangé au.*

up the rest of the day. Even allowing for the obstacles put in their way, Fabre, Chabot and the rest did not come out of this very well. Cambon's evidence carried conviction – it still does – and Herman had nothing more to do than to allow justice to take its course. For him and for Fouquier it had been a good day. The accused rather spoiled things in the late afternoon by demanding to call their own witnesses. Fouquier, who could scarcely deny them their legal right, duly noted down the names in a list of 'witnesses to be called'. He must have looked at it with despair for it included the mayor of Paris, the Foreign Minister and a dozen deputies, amongst whom were Lindet and Robespierre. Lindet's intrepid honesty might well lead him to defend the accused and expose the division within the Committee of Public Safety while there was no knowing what might not result from a confrontation between Robespierre and Danton. Obviously nothing of the sort must be allowed to happen, but Fouquier thought it was up to someone else to stop it.

On 3 April Danton had to be given a hearing and he seems to have spoken almost all day. The *Bulletin,* which reported the first and third days of the trial at some length, was curiously reticent when it came to recording Danton's remarks and Topino-Lebrun jotted down only his more memorable outbursts. Michelet may have exaggerated the intelligence, if not the machiavellianism, of the editors of the *Bulletin* whom he accused of mentioning Danton's violent outbursts out of context, to suggest that they were the fits of temper of a man who could not reply to the charges against him. They do preserve enough of the genuine Danton to suggest that some of the more apocryphal remarks attributed to him were at least in character. Accusation and defence covered the whole of Danton's revolutionary career. He declared his intention of refuting Saint-Just clause by clause and his own argument seems to have followed the rambling pattern of Saint-Just's report. What mattered to the court was not so much Danton's unverifiable refutation of charges too general to admit of proof or disproof, but the vindication of his career as a whole and the impression he was able to convey of the wounded lion turning on a jackal pack. If anything could make any difference it would be that.

From the moment Danton began to speak, the whole trial took on a new tragic dimension. The man with Shakespeare on his shelves assumed the proportions of Coriolanus and the accents of Antony.

> My voice, so often heard in the people's cause . . . will not find it hard to repulse calumny. Will the cowards who are slandering me dare to attack me to my face? Let them show themselves and I shall soon cover them with all their natural disgrace and opprobrium. I have said it already and I repeat: my domicile will soon be in oblivion and my name in the Pantheon . . . Here is my head to answer for everything . . . Life is a burden to me. I am impatient to be rid of it.

Throughout that long day his mood fluctuated. He knew enough about revolutionary justice to know what the odds against him were. Taking his condemnation for granted, he could speak with the accents of a tragic hero.

> During the past two days the court has got to know Danton. Tomorrow he hopes to sleep in the bosom of glory. He has never asked for pardon and you will see him fly to the scaffold with his usual serenity and the calm of a clear conscience.

There were times, though, when he was almost convinced, by the force of his own anger and its visible effects on the audience, that he might have a chance. As Pâris put it, 'Fouquier and his worthy friend, Fleuriot, frightful as they were, judges and jury, all were shattered by men like this and the witness [i.e. Pâris] thought for a moment that they would not have the audacity to sacrifice them'. Danton's range extended from furious anger to blistering irony.

> I must speak of the three petty knaves [*plats coquins*] who have destroyed Robespierre. I have vital evidence to reveal; I demand an undisturbed hearing. The nation's safety makes that imperative. . . . It is very strange how blind the Convention has been about me until today; the way in which it has suddenly seen the light is positively miraculous.

There is no point in trying to reconstitute the speech from the fragments that have been preserved, or to judge it as legal evidence. The accusation amounted to the charge that Danton's whole career had been one of personal ambition that required monarchy for its satisfaction. His defence amounted to a denial of everything. Those who have read this book so far must come to their own conclusion. One of the most brilliant aspects of Danton's long improvisation was his skill in concealing what was better not investigated, and even turning it to his own advantage. To the charge that he allowed the Prussian army to escape after Valmy, he replied that the man he sent to keep an eye on Dumouriez was Billaud-Varenne. When he gave Billaud 6,000 livres for his expenses he asked for no accounts – but 'Billaud-Varenne cannot forgive me for having been my secretary'. Sometimes Danton went too far for credibility, as when he claimed that he and Westermann had nothing in common, but when reading his 'defence' (it was more in the nature of an attack) it is difficult to keep in mind the tortuous and ambiguous career that actually lay behind it. The real question had nothing to do with legal charges and their refutation. It was all a question of politics, as it had always been with Danton, and the issue was whether the republic would be in better keeping in his hands, with all his faults, than in those of the committees, with all theirs. The answer is no clearer now than it was then. Of one thing there could be no doubt: Danton was converting his audience. Herman and Fouquier were professionals who knew what was expected of them – and what they could expect if they failed to produce it – but the precious fiction of impartial revolutionary justice would make it very hard for the government to punish the jurors if they delivered the wrong verdict. As the afternoon wore on and the public voiced its sympathy with Danton, this began to appear quite possible. The *Bulletin* records unctuously that the judges, taking pity on Danton's exhaustion, invited him to take some rest. This is scarcely the tone of the note Herman passed to Fouquier: 'In half an hour I will suspend Danton's defence'. According to Pâris, Danton only agreed to stop in return for a promise that he would be allowed to resume on the following day.

Fouquier told d'Aubigny that, either that night or the previous one, he went round to the Committee of Public Safety with his list of witnesses. Robespierre had gone home and Billaud and Saint-Just told him there was no question of any defence witnesses being called. When Fouquier insisted, they threatened him. He probably did not insist very much. On the third day of the trial he told Danton that, in the name of justice and humanity, he had asked the committee's permission for witnesses to be called.

Danton replied that it was not a question of justice and humanity but of legal rights. According to d'Aubigny, he accused Robespierre, Couthon, Saint-Just, Barère, Billaud, Amar, Voulland and especially Vadier, and 'the public, with loud cries, insisted that Danton's witnesses be called'. By now Danton was demanding not merely his witnesses but the appointment by the Assembly of a commission to receive his denunciation of his opponents. Buffeted between Saint-Just and Billaud on the one hand and Danton on the other, Fouquier and Herman wrote to the Committee of Public Safety:

> A terrible storm has been raging since the session began. The accused are frantically demanding the hearing of their witnesses. [Sixteen deputies were named, who did not correspond to those on Fouquier's list.] The accused are denouncing to the people what they say is the rejection of their demand. In spite of the firmness of the president and of the entire court, their repeated demands are disturbing the session and they are proclaiming that, short of a decree [by the Assembly] they will not be quiet until their witnesses have been heard. We invite you to prescribe formally what our conduct should be concerning this request since judicial procedure gives us no motive for rejecting it.

That at least disposed of their own responsibility.

Danton then demanded the right to resume his defence but was told by Herman that he would have to wait until the remainder of the accused had been interrogated. There followed a disjointed exchange with several of the prisoners, touching on many issues and producing evasions from some and more or less convincing explanations from others, but elucidating nothing in depth. Delacroix, who showed more spirit than the rest, returned to the question of the witnesses. 'For the past three days I have been demanding in vain the sacred right of an accused to his defence . . . I challenge the public prosecutor to declare in the face of the people, the witness to my attempts to clear myself, why I am refused this legitimate satisfaction.' Fouquier tried to evade this by claiming that he was not opposed to the convocation of witnesses and it was up to Delacroix to produce them. Further pursued by Delacroix, he eventually agreed to convene the witnesses – with the exception of deputies, on the disingenuous

171

ground that the Assembly as a whole was in the rôle of accuser. To this Delacroix replied that, as he understood it, his colleagues were allowed to assassinate him but he was not permitted to expose them. Much against his will, Fouquier agreed to consult the Assembly again – in fact, he addressed his letter not to the Convention but to the Committee of Public Safety. He then accused Danton of having opposed the insurrection of 31 May. When Danton denied this and offered to produce witnesses to prove it, Fouquier, who was making heavy weather of things, turned back to Delacroix and Philippeaux. When he insinuated that Philippeaux's defence did not correspond to his actions, he got the reply, 'You are authorised to have me killed but not to insult me'.

After some further exchanges, Amar and Voulland returned to the court with a decree from the Convention. According to Pâris they were pale with fright and anger. Amar said to Fouquier, 'This is what you want', and Fouquier, smiling with relief, said it was badly needed. One can understand his point of view. On receipt of his letter, Saint-Just had gone to the Assembly and, instead of reading out what Fouquier had actually written, had told the deputies that the prisoners were in revolt against the court. To make doubly sure, he and Billaud announced the discovery of a prison plot, organised by Desmoulins' wife and General Dillon, to rescue the accused and murder the Committee of Public Safety. This rested entirely on the evidence of one prisoner, Laflotte, who was soon afterwards to be convicted of perjury when he manufactured evidence in another case. The docile Convention agreed to arrest Lucile Desmoulins and voted that prisoners who insulted the revolutionary tribunal should be removed from the court and tried in their absence.

When this was read out in court, Danton was quick to call the public to witness that none of the accused had insulted the court, but Desmoulins was overcome by the news of his wife's arrest and all the accused understood that they had nothing more to hope for from the Convention. Fouquier now felt confident enough to announce that he would refrain from calling his crowd of prosecution witnesses and the accused would likewise not be allowed to summon theirs. It was a curious conception of fair play. This time he had won. It is not clear whether the court rose immediately after the receipt of the message from the Assembly or whether the aimless interrogation continued a little longer. The accused were hamstrung and the trial had now lasted for three days.

On 5 April the session opened at 8.30 instead of the usual time of 10 o'clock, presumably to forestall the crowds. Fouquier immediately asked the jurors if they had heard enough to make up their minds. Bullied by Herman, Fouquier and the men from the Committee of General Security, they agreed. At this point the prisoners began a noisy demonstration and were removed from the court in accordance with the provisions of the decree voted on the previous day. According to Pâris the jury was away for about two hours and a rumour spread through the court that the accused had been acquitted. Courtois claimed that three of them, Topino-Lebrun, Trinchard and Sambat, told David they believed the prisoners to be innocent – but Sambat, although one of the regular jurors, was not involved in this particular trial.[29] Topino-Lebrun said the jurors were shown a letter from abroad, addressed to Danton. If this had proved anything it would presumably have been produced in open court. It was probably the letter from Bâle that Fouquier had requested from the Foreign Office on 3 April.[30] If so, it had nothing to do with Danton and merely said that the local counter-revolutionaries had been dismayed when they heard of Chabot's arrest. Mathiez wondered whether the letter in question might not have been the much more incriminating one from Whitehall to the banker, Perregaux, proving that the British Government had its paid agents in the Jacobin Club.[31] This letter is now filed with Danton's papers and if it had been addressed to him it might well have impressed any jury. It was, however, addressed to Perregaux, who had been investigated and cleared by Cambon. The actual evidence did not matter very much since the question facing the jury was as political as the trial itself. As the juror, Souberbielle said to Topino, 'This is not a trial but a [political] act . . . We are not jurors but *statesmen* . . . The two are impossible and one must perish . . . Do you want to kill Robespierre? No. Well that alone means that you have just condemned Danton.'[32] It was perhaps not a very judicial way of

29. *Réponse aux détracteurs du 9 thermidor*, Paris, an IV, p. 36 note 28.
30. Archives Nationales, W 173.
31. *La conspiration de l'étranger*, Paris, 1918, p. 137.
32. J. Claretie, *Camille Desmoulins, Lucile Desmoulins*, Paris, 1875, p. 332.

looking at things but it was a fair summary of the situation. In the end the jury returned verdicts of guilty against all the accused except Lulier. If he knew why he was acquitted, no one does now.

Danton could hardly have been surprised by the verdict, and, as he had told the court, he was not afraid of death. Riouffe, who was in the same prison, said he overheard Danton swearing a good deal and talking, ostensibly to Westermann who was in the next cell, but actually to the public and to posterity. 'I'm leaving everything in a frightful mess. There's not one of them who knows anything about government . . . If I left my balls to Robespierre and my legs to Couthon [a paralytic] the Committee of Public Safety could last a bit longer.'[33] According to Riouffe, he spoke a good deal about trees and nature. In the end, Falstaff had taken over from Mark Antony.

The accounts of Danton's last hours are various and conflicting.[34] Perhaps as accurate as any are the recollections of an eyewitness, Arnault, though he wrote them down much later.

> Danton was the last to appear on the platform, soaked with the blood of his friends. Night was falling. At the foot of the horrible statue [of liberty] whose mass stood out against the sky in a dreadful silhouette, I saw, like a shade from Dante, the tribune standing, dimly lit by the dying sun, as though emerging from the tomb instead of about to enter it . . . Time cannot erase the horrible pantomime from my memory. I recall the full force of my feeling at Danton's last words, which I did not hear myself but which were passed round with horror and admiration: 'Above all, don't forget to show my head to the people: it's worth seeing.'

33. Riouffe, *Mémoires d'un détenu,* Paris, an III, p. 71.
34. See A. Aulard, 'Derniers moments et exécution de Danton' in *Etudes et leçons sur la Révolution française,* 9th series, Paris, 1924.

Bibliographical Note

This guide to further reading is intended merely as orientation for anyone wanting to find out more about Danton for himself. To cover the 'Dantonists' as a whole and the political battles in which they engaged would require a general bibliography of the French Revolution quite beyond the proportions of a book of this kind. With occasional exceptions, I have therefore listed only those works directly relating to Danton himself that seem to me particularly important. I have omitted many that deal only with particular details of his career, to which I have referred in my text. All the works in French were published in Paris.

Unpublished sources
There is not much in the Archives Nationales that is directly relevant to Danton. His few papers are divided between F⁷ 4434 (which includes Chabot's letters to him) and AF II 49, containing the letter from Whitehall to Perregaux. Fouquier-Tinville's papers on Danton's trial are in W 173 and W 342. More revealing are the records of the trial of Fouquier-Tinville himself, in W 501. The correspondence of Danton and the other representatives on mission in Belgium in 1792–3 is in DS2.

Contemporary printed sources
Danton's speeches have been edited by A. Fribourg (*Discours de Danton*, 1910). Apart from the *Moniteur*, the most important newspapers are Desmoulins' *Vieux Cordelier* (ed. H. Calvet, 1936) and the *Bulletin du Tribunal révolutionnaire*. The memoirs of R. Levasseur (3 vols, 1831) and D.-J. Garat (1862) are particularly important. Evidence of Danton's payment by the court is to be found in B. de Moleville, *Private Memoirs relative to the last years of the reign of Louis XVI* (London, 1797), Bacourt, *Correspondance entre le comte de Mirabeau et le comte de La Marck* (3 vols, 1851), and *The memoirs of La Fayette* (6 vols, 1837–8). The memoirs of Louis-Philippe (1973) contain the future king's own account of his meeting with Danton in the autumn of 1792. Robinet, *Notes de Topino-Lebrun sur le procès*

de Danton (1875) is essential reading for Danton's trial. Useful material on particular aspects of Danton's career can be found in E.-B. Courtois, *Lettre à l'auteur du Patriote Français* (n.p. undated, but 1791) and in Villain d'Aubigny, *Principaux événements pour et contre la Révolution* (an III). Couthon's correspondence (ed. F. Mège, 1872) offers hints on the attitude of the Committee of Public Safety towards Danton in the spring of 1794.

Secondary works

M.-N. Villiaumé, *Histoire de la Révolution française* (4 vols, 1850), although not specifically concerned with Danton, played an important part in his rehabilitation. This process was carried to the point of canonisation by A. Bougeart, *Danton* (1861) and Dr Robinet, *Le Procès des Dantonistes* (1879), *Danton, Mémoire sur sa vie privée* (1884), *Danton, émigré* (1887), and *Danton, Homme d'état* (1889). Both Bougeart and Robinet reprint many of the most important documents. J. Claretie, *Camille Desmoulins, Lucile Desmoulins, Etude sur les Dantonistes* (1875) is equally sympathetic. The opposite point of view was presented by A. Mathiez. His most important works, so far as Danton is concerned, are *Le Club des Cordeliers pendant la crise de Varennes et le massacre du Champ de Mars* (1910), *Danton et la paix* (1919), *La corruption parlementaire sous la Terreur* (1917), *La conspiration de l'étranger* (1918), *Un procès de corruption sous la Terreur: l'affair de la Compagnie des Indes* (1920), and *Autour de Danton* (1926). Most of these books consisted of reprinted articles. Since Mathiez began his attack on Danton there have been a fair number of biographies, none of them breaking much new ground. The most useful are those by L. Madelin (1914) and L. Barthou (1932) and, more recently, J. Hérissay, *Cet excellent M. Danton* (1960). Chabot's story of a foreign plot has been investigated by A. de Lestapis (*La 'conspiration de Batz' (1793–1794)*, 1969) with results that are very interesting but not quite conclusive.

Articles

The most important sources of information about Danton are the articles published by A. Aulard in *La Révolution française* and by A. Mathiez in the *Annales Révolutionnaires* which later became the *Annales historiques de la Révolution française*. Most of

Aulard's work was reprinted in the various series of his *Etudes et leçons sur la Révolution française,* and the more important of Mathiez's contributions were collected in the works mentioned above. In addition to *Les comptes de Danton* and *Encore les comptes de Danton* (1888 and 1889) and *La diplomatie du premier Comité de Salut Public* (1890), Aulard produced what amounted to a biography of Danton in seven articles that appeared in the *Révolution française* in 1893: 'Danton au District des Cordeliers et à la Commune de Paris', 'Danton au Club des Cordeliers et au Département de Paris', 'Danton en 1791 et 1792', 'Danton et la révolution du 10 août 1792', 'Danton à la Convention'. His 'Derniers moments et exécution de Danton' also appeared in the *Révolution française,* in 1922. He also published 'L'enfance et la jeunesse de Danton' in the *Revue Encyclopédique* in 1893. Other useful articles that appeared in the *Revolution française* are Robinet, 'Notes et souvenirs de Courtois' (1887) and P. Caron, 'Danton et les massacres de septembre' (1931).

In addition to Mathiez's contributions, too numerous to list individually, E. Campagnac, 'Quelques récits parus dans *L'Echo d'Arcis* sur des épisodes de la vie de Danton' (*Annales historiques de la Révolution française* (1952) is useful on Danton's early life. Two other articles from the same review are of outstanding importance: G. Lefebvre, 'Sur Danton' (1932) and G. Pioro, 'Sur la fortune de Danton' (1955).

C. Becker 'A letter from Danton to Marie Antoinette' (*American Historical Review,* 1921) is of some interest, although Lefebvre was probably right in thinking the letter itself to be a forgery.

Index